ENDANGERED AND THREATENED WILDLIFE AND PLANTS - STATUS FOR OREGON SPOTTED FROG (US FISH AND WILDLIFE SERVICE REGULATION) (FWS) (2018 EDITION)

Updated as of May 29, 2018

THE LAW LIBRARY

TABLE OF CONTENTS

AGENCY	4
ACTION	4
SUMMARY	4
DATES	4
ADDRESSES	4
FOR FURTHER INFORMATION CONTACT	4
SUPPLEMENTARY INFORMATION	5
Executive Summary	5
Previous Federal Actions	5
Background	6
Summary of Factors Affecting the Species	21
Summary of Comments and Recommendations	69
Summary of Changes From the Proposed Rule	89
Determination	89
Available Conservation Measures	92
Required Determinations	95
References Cited	95
Authors	96
LIST OF SUBJECTS IN 50 CFR PART 17	96
Regulation Promulgation	96
REGULATORY TEXT	96
PART 17 AMENDED	96
Authority:	96
§ 17.11 Endangered and threatened wildlife.	96

AGENCY

Fish and Wildlife Service, Interior.

ACTION

Final rule.

SUMMARY

We, the U.S. Fish and Wildlife Service (Service), determine threatened species status under the Endangered Species Act of 1973 (Act), as amended, for Oregon spotted frog (Rana pretiosa), an amphibian species from British Columbia, Washington, Oregon, and California. The effect of this regulation will be to add this species to the List of Endangered and Threatened Wildlife.

DATES

This rule is effective September 29, 2014.

ADDRESSES

This final rule is available on the Internet at http://www.regulations.gov and http://www.fws.gov/wafwo/osf.html. Comments and materials we received, as well as some of the supporting documentation we used in preparing this rule, are available for public inspection at http://www.regulations.gov. All of the comments, materials, and documentation that we considered in this rulemaking are available by appointment, during normal business hours at: U.S. Fish and Wildlife Service, Washington Fish and Wildlife Office, 510 Desmond Drive SE., Suite 102, Lacey, WA 98503; by telephone at 360-753-9440; or by facsimile at 360-753-9445.

FOR FURTHER INFORMATION CONTACT

Ken Berg, Manager, U.S. Fish and Wildlife Service, Washington Fish and Wildlife Office, 510 Desmond Drive SE., Suite 102, Lacey, WA 98503; telephone 360-753-9440; facsimile 360-753-9445. Persons who use a telecommunications device for the deaf (TDD) may call the Federal Information Relay Service (FIRS) at 800-877-8339.

SUPPLEMENTARY INFORMATION

Executive Summary

Why we need to publish a rule. Under the Endangered Species Act, a species may warrant protection through listing if it is endangered or threatened throughout all or a significant portion of its range. Listing a species as an endangered or threatened species can only be completed by issuing a rule.

This rule will finalize the listing of the Oregon spotted frog (Rana pretiosa) as a threatened species.

The basis for our action. Under the Endangered Species Act, we can determine that a species is an endangered or threatened species based on any of five factors: (A) The present or threatened destruction, modification, or curtailment of its habitat or range; (B) overutilization for commercial, recreational, scientific, or educational purposes; (C) disease or predation; (D) the inadequacy of existing regulatory mechanisms; or (E) other natural or manmade factors affecting its continued existence. We have determined that the Oregon spotted frog is impacted by one or more of the following factors:

- Habitat necessary to support all life stages continues to be impacted or destroyed by human activities that result in the loss of wetlands to land conversions; hydrologic changes resulting from operation of existing water diversions/manipulation structures, new and existing residential and road developments, drought, and removal of beavers; changes in water temperature and vegetation structure resulting from reed canarygrass invasions, plant succession, and restoration plantings; and increased sedimentation, increased water temperatures, reduced water quality, and vegetation changes resulting from the timing and intensity of livestock grazing (or in some instances, removal of livestock grazing at locations where it maintains early seral stage habitat essential for breeding).

- Predation by nonnative species, including nonnative trout and bullfrogs.

- Inadequate existing regulatory mechanisms that result in significant negative impacts, such as habitat loss and modification.

- Other natural or manmade factors including small and isolated breeding locations, low connectivity, low genetic diversity within occupied sub-basins, and genetic differentiation between sub-basins.

Peer review and public comment. We sought comments from independent specialists to ensure that our designation is based on scientifically sound data, assumptions, and analyses. We invited these peer reviewers to comment on our listing proposal. We also considered all comments and information we received during the comment period.

Previous Federal Actions

On August 29, 2013, we published a proposed rule (78 FR 53582) to list the Oregon spotted frog as a threatened species under the Act (16 U.S.C. 1531 et seq.). Please refer to that proposed rule for a detailed description of Federal actions concerning this species. Also on August 29, 2013, we proposed to designate critical habitat for the Oregon spotted frog (78 FR 53538). On September 26, 2013, we published a document (78 FR 59334) extending the comment period of both proposed rules and announcing a public hearing on the proposals to list and designate critical habitat for this species.

This rule concerns only the listing of the Oregon spotted frog; we will make a final determination concerning critical habitat for the Oregon spotted frog in the near future.

Background

The Oregon spotted frog is named for the characteristic black spots covering the head, back, sides, and legs. The dark spots have ragged edges and light centers, usually associated with a tubercle or raised area of skin. The coloration patterns on Oregon spotted frogs all develop with age; the spots become larger and darker and the edges become more ragged as the individual gets older (Hayes 1994, p. 14). Overall body color also varies with age. Juveniles are usually brown or, occasionally, olive green on the back and white, cream, or flesh-colored with reddish pigments on the underlegs and abdomen developing with age (McAllister and Leonard 1997, pp. 1-2). Adults range from brown to reddish brown but tend to become redder with age. Large, presumably older, individuals may be brick red over most of the dorsal (back) surfaces (McAllister and Leonard 1997, pp. 1-2). Red surface pigments on the adult abdomen also expand with age, and the underlegs of adults become a vivid orange red. Tan to orange folds along the sides of the back (dorsolateral folds) extend from behind the eye to midway along the back (McAllister and Leonard 1997, p. 1). The eyes are upturned; there is a faint mask, and a light jaw stripe extends to the shoulder. Small bumps and tubercles usually cover the back and sides (Leonard et al. 1993, p. 130). The hind legs are short relative to body length, and the hind feet are fully webbed (Leonard et al. 1993, p. 130).

The Oregon spotted frog is a medium-sized frog that ranges from about 1.7 to 4.1 inches (in) (44 to 105 millimeters (mm)) in body length (McAllister and Leonard 1997, p. 1; Rombough et al. 2006, p. 210). Females are typically larger than males; females reach up to 105 mm (4 in) (Rombough et al. 2006, p. 210) and males to 75 mm (3 in) (Leonard et al. 1993, p. 130).

Morphological characters can be used to distinguish Oregon spotted frogs from other closely related spotted frogs. Mottling with dark pigments and fragmentation of the superficial red or orange-red wash on the abdomen can distinguish the Oregon spotted frog from some Columbia spotted frog populations (Hayes 1997, p. 3; Hayes et al. 1997, p. 1). Other characteristics, such as coloration of the underlegs and abdomen, size and shapes of spots, groin mottling, eye positions, relative length of hind legs to body size, degree of webbing, and behaviors can be used to distinguish Oregon spotted frogs from adults of closely related species. Tadpoles are more difficult to differentiate from other species (Corkran and Thoms 1996, p. 150; McAllister and Leonard 1997, p. 6).

The Oregon spotted frog has a weak call consisting of a rapid series of six to nine low clucking notes described as sounding like a distant woodpecker's tapping. Males will call at any time, both day and night (McAllister and Leonard 1997, p. 12). Males have been documented to call from submerged sites that are physically distant (tens to hundreds of meters) from oviposition (egg-laying) sites (Bowerman 2010, p. 85). These submerged calls are inaudible at the surface and begin several days prior to breeding. Submerged calling is more frequent at night, although daytime calling has been recorded during overcast days (Bowerman 2010, pp. 85-86). It is unclear if mate selection takes place during this period of calling remotely from the breeding site, but it seems likely (Bowerman 2010, p. 86). This species rarely vocalizes except during the breeding season (Leonard et al. 1993, p. 132); however, vocalizations have been heard during the fall (Leonard et al. 1997, pp. 73-74; Pearl 2010, pers. comm.).

Taxonomy

The scientific name Rana pretiosa (order Anura; family Ranidae) was first applied to a series of five specimens collected in 1841 from the vicinity of Puget Sound (Baird and Girard 1853, p. 378). Two of these specimens were later determined to be northern red-legged frogs (Rana aurora) (Hayes 1994, p. 4; Green et al. 1997, p. 4). Dunlap (1955) demonstrated the morphological differences between northern red-legged frogs, Cascades frogs, and spotted frogs. Subsequently, the "spotted frog" was separated into two species, Rana pretiosa (Oregon spotted frog) and Rana luteiventris (Columbia spotted frog) based on genetic analyses (Green et al. 1996, 1997).

In 2008, phylogenetic analyses were conducted on samples of Oregon spotted frogs collected from 3 locations in Washington and 13 locations in Oregon (Funk et al. 2008). Results indicate two well-supported clades (a group of biological taxa (as species) that includes all descendants of one common ancestor) nested within the Oregon spotted frog: The Columbia clade (Trout Lake Natural Area Preserve (NAP) and Camas Prairie) and the southern Oregon clade (Wood River and Buck Lake in the Klamath Basin). The two sites that comprise the Columbia clade occur on opposite sides of the Columbia River in Washington (Trout Lake NAP) and in Oregon (Camas Prairie). Haplotype and nucleotide diversity was low for Oregon spotted frogs in general and was very low for each of the two nested clades, respectively (Funk et al. 2008, p. 203). Only six haplotypes were found across the entire range of the Oregon spotted frog, indicating low genetic variation (Funk et al. 2008, p. 205). Recent genetic work conducted by Robertson and Funk (2012, p. 6) in the Deschutes and Klamath basins indicate the sampled Oregon spotted frog sites are characterized by very small effective population sizes and little genetic variation (i.e., measured as low heterozygosity and low allelic richness).

Blouin et al. (2010) performed genetic analyses on Oregon spotted frogs from 23 of the known sites in British Columbia, Washington, and Oregon for variation at 13 microsatellite loci and 298 base pairs of mitochondrial DNA. Their results indicate that Rana pretiosa comprised six major genetic groups: (1) British Columbia; (2) the Chehalis drainage in Washington, (3) the Columbia drainage in Washington, (4) Camas Prairie in northern Oregon, (5) the central Cascades of Oregon, and (6) the Klamath basin (Blouin et al. 2010, pp. 2184-2185). Within the northern genetic groups, the British Columbia (Lower Fraser River) and Chehalis (Black River) populations form the next natural grouping (Blouin et al. 2010, p. 2189). Recently discovered locales in the Sumas, South Fork Nooksack, and Samish Rivers occur in-between these two groups. While no genetic testing has been done on these newly found populations, it is reasonable to assume that they are likely to be closely related to either the British Columbia or Chehalis group, or both, given their proximity and use of similar lowland marsh habitats.

Levels of genetic variation in the Oregon spotted frog groups are low compared to other ranid frogs, suggesting these populations are very small and/or very isolated (Blouin et al. 2010, p. 2184). Blouin et al. (2010) found a high frequency of private alleles in the mitochondrial DNA (i.e., an allele found in only one population or geographic location) in the central Cascades and Klamath Basin groups. This finding suggests an historical (rather than recent) isolation between individual groups (Blouin et al. 2010, p. 2189). This finding also reinforces microsatellite-based conclusions that gene flow among sites has been very low, even on small geographic scales (Blouin et al. 2010, p. 2188). Recent work by Robertson and Funk (2012) in the Deschutes and

Klamath basins reinforces the Blouin et al. (2010) findings. Due to Oregon spotted frogs' highly aquatic habits, connectivity between Oregon spotted frog sites depends on the connectivity of streams, rivers, and lakes. Gene flow (based on both microsatellite and mitochondrial analyses) is extremely low beyond 6 miles (mi) (10 kilometers (km)) (Blouin et al. 2010, pp. 2186, 2188), and most Oregon spotted frog populations are separated by more than 6.2 mi (10 km). Therefore, Blouin et al. (2010, p. 2189) and Robertson and Funk (2012, p. 5) hypothesize that low aquatic connectivity and small isolated populations are important causes of the low genetic diversity within sites and the high genetic differentiation among sites.

Life History

Male Oregon spotted frogs are not territorial and often gather in large groups of 25 or more individuals at specific locations (Leonard et al. 1993, p. 132). Breeding occurs in February or March at lower elevations and between early April and early June at higher elevations (Leonard et al. 1993, p. 132). Males and females separate soon after egg-laying, with females returning to fairly solitary lives. Males often stay at the breeding site, possibly for several weeks, until egg-laying is completed (McAllister and Leonard 1997, p. 13). (The terms "egg-laying site" or "egg-laying habitat" are used interchangeably with "breeding site," "breeding area," or "breeding habitat" throughout this rule). Breeding site, breeding area, and breeding location terminology refer to geographic areas where concentrated breeding has been observed.

Oregon spotted frogs' eggs are extremely vulnerable to desiccation and freezing as a result of the species' laying habits. Females may deposit their egg masses at the same locations in successive years, indicating the sites may have unique characteristics. For example, some marked males and females at Sunriver (Upper Deschutes River, Oregon) returned to the same breeding site for 3 or more years (Bowerman 2006, pers. comm.). Further, at several sites in Oregon and Washington, the same egg-laying locations have been used for more than a decade (Hayes 2008, pers. comm.; Hallock 2012, pp. 24-27). Although egg masses are occasionally laid singly, the majority of egg masses are laid communally in groups of a few to several hundred (Licht 1971, p. 119; Nussbaum et al. 1983, p. 186; Cook 1984, p. 87; Hayes et al. 1997 p. 3; Engler and Friesz 1998, p. 3). They are laid in shallow, often temporary, pools of water; on gradually receding shorelines; on benches of seasonal lakes and marshes; and in wet meadows. These sites are usually associated with the previous year's emergent vegetation and are generally no more than 14 in. (35 centimeters (cm.)) deep (Pearl and Hayes 2004, pp. 19-20). Most of these sites dry up later in the season (Engler 1999, pers. comm.), but are connected via surface water to permanently wetted areas, such as creeks, wetlands, and springs. Shallow water is easily warmed by the sun, and warmth hastens egg development (McAllister and Leonard 1997, p. 8). However, laying eggs in shallow water can result in high mortality rates for eggs and hatchling larvae due to desiccation or freezing.

Licht (1974, pp. 617-625) documented the highly variable mortality rates for spotted frog life-history stages in marsh areas in the lower Fraser Valley, British Columbia, embryos (30 percent), tadpoles (99 percent), and post-metamorphic (after the change from tadpole to adult, or "metamorphosis") frogs (95 percent). Licht (1974, p. 625) estimated mortality of each life stage and predicted only a 1 percent chance of survival of eggs to metamorphosis, a 67 percent chance of juvenile survival for the first year, and a 64 percent adult annual survival with males having a higher mortality rate than females. An average adult between-year survival of 37 percent was estimated by a mark-recapture study at Dempsey Creek in Washington between 1997 and 1999 (Watson et al. 2000, p. 19).

Adult Oregon spotted frogs begin to breed by 1 to 3 years of age, depending on sex, elevation, and latitude. Males may breed at 1 year at lower elevations and latitudes but generally breed at 2 years of age. Females breed by 2 or 3 years of age, depending on elevation and latitude. Longevity of the species is not well understood; however, there are multiple examples of Oregon spotted frogs living beyond 7 years of age (Watson et al. 2000, p. 21; McAllister 2008, pers. comm.; Oertley 2005, pers. comm.; Pearl 2005, pers. comm.).

Egg-laying can begin as early as February in lowland areas of British Columbia and Washington and as late as early June in the higher elevations. Tadpoles metamorphose into froglets (tiny frogs) (about 0.6-1.75 in. (16-43 mm.) in length) during their first summer (Leonard et al. 1993, p. 132; Pearl and Bowerman 2005, pers. comm.). Tadpoles are grazers, having rough tooth rows for scraping plant surfaces and ingesting plant tissue and bacteria. They also consume algae, detritus, and probably carrion (Licht 1974, p. 624; McAllister and Leonard 1997, p. 13).

Post-metamorphic Oregon spotted frogs are opportunistic predators that prey on live animals, primarily insects, found in or near the water. Prey groups of adult frogs include leaf beetles (Chrysomelidae), ground beetles (Carabidae), spiders (Arachnida), rove beetles (Staphylinidae), syrphid flies (Syrphidae), long-legged flies (Dolichopodidae), ants (Formicidae), water striders (Gerridae), spittlebugs (Cercopidae), leaf hoppers (Cicadellidae), aphids (Aphididae), dragonflies and damsel flies (Odonates), and yellowjackets (Vespidae) (Licht 1986a, pp. 27-28). Oregon spotted frogs also eat adult Pacific tree frogs (Pseudacris regilla), small red-legged frogs, and newly metamorphosed red-legged frogs and western toad (Anaxyrus boreas) juveniles (Licht 1986a, p. 28; Pearl and Hayes 2002, pp. 145-147; Pearl et al. 2005a, p. 37).

Similar to many North American pond-breeding anurans (belonging to the Order Anura, which contains all frogs), predators can strongly affect the abundance of larval and post-metamorphic Oregon spotted frogs. The heaviest losses to predation are thought to occur shortly after tadpoles emerge from eggs, when they are relatively exposed and poor swimmers (Licht 1974, p. 624). However, the odds of survival appear to increase as tadpoles grow in size and aquatic vegetation matures, thus affording cover (Licht 1974, p. 624). Adult Oregon spotted frogs have a number of documented and potential natural predators, including garter snakes (Thamnophis species (spp.)), great blue herons (Ardea herodias), green herons (Butorides virescens), American bitterns (Botaurus lentiginosus), belted kingfishers (Ceryle alcyon), sandhill cranes (Grus canadensis), raccoons (Procyon lotor), coyotes (Canis latrans), striped skunks (Mephitis mephitis), mink (Neovison vison), river otters (Lontra canadensis), and feral cats (Felis domesticus) (McAllister and Leonard 1997, p. 13; Hayes et al. 2005, p. 307; Hayes et al. 2006, p. 209). Tadpoles may be preyed upon by numerous vertebrate predators including belted kingfishers, hooded mergansers (Lophodytes cucullatus), common garter snakes (Thamnophis sirtalis), western terrestrial garter snakes (Thamnophis elegans), larval and adult roughskin newts (Taricha granulosa), larval northwestern salamanders (Ambystoma gracile), cutthroat trout (Oncorhynchus clarki), Olympic mudminnows (Novumbra hubbsi), and three-spined sticklebacks (Gasterosteus aculeatus) (McAllister and Leonard 1997, p. 14).

Subadult Oregon spotted frogs have been observed within dense aggregations of recently hatched Oregon spotted frog tadpoles, and stomach flushing verified that these subadult Oregon spotted frogs had consumed (cannibalized) recently hatched conspecific (belonging to the same species) tadpoles (McAllister 2008, pers. comm.). Invertebrate predators include dytiscid beetles (Dytiscus spp.), giant water bugs (Lethocerus americanus), backswimmers (Notonecta undulata and N. kirbyi), water scorpions (Ranatra sp.), dragonfly nymphs (Odonata), and worm-leeches (Arhynchobdellida) (McAllister and Leonard 1997, p. 14). Leeches and other invertebrates, roughskin newts, and northwestern salamanders are likely Oregon spotted frog egg predators (Licht 1974, p. 622).

The introduction of nonnative species into the historical range of the Oregon spotted frog is believed to have contributed to the decline of this and other species of frogs (Hayes and Jennings

1986, pp. 491-492, 494-496; Hayes 1994, p. 5; 61 FR 25813; McAllister and Leonard 1997, pp. 25-26; Pearl et al. 2004, pp. 17-18). American bullfrogs (Lithobates catesbeianus) are known predators of Oregon spotted frogs (R. Haycock and R.A. Woods, unpubl. data, 2001 cited in COSFRT 2012, p. 19), and introduced fish such as brook trout (Salvelinus fontinalis) and centrarchids (Micropterus and Lepomis spp.) are also likely predators (Pearl et al. 2009a, p. 140).

Habitat

Watson et al. (2003, p. 298) summarized the conditions required for completion of the Oregon spotted frog's life cycle as shallow water areas for egg and tadpole survival; perennially deep, moderately vegetated pools for adult and juvenile survival in the dry season; and perennial water for protecting all age classes during cold wet weather.

The Oregon spotted frog inhabits emergent wetland habitats in forested landscapes, although it is not typically found under forest canopy. Historically, this species was also associated with lakes in the prairie landscape of the Puget lowlands (McAllister and Leonard 1997, p. 16). This is the most aquatic native frog species in the Pacific Northwest (PNW), as all other species have a terrestrial life stage. It is found in or near a perennial body of water, such as a spring, pond, lake, sluggish stream, irrigation canal, or roadside ditch (Engler 1999, pers. comm.). The observation that extant Oregon spotted frog populations tend to occur in larger wetlands led Hayes (1994, Part II pp. 5, 7) to hypothesize that a minimum size of 9 acres (ac) (4 hectares (ha)) may be necessary to reach suitably warm temperatures and support a large enough population to persist despite high predation rates. However, Oregon spotted frogs also occupy smaller sites and are known to occur at sites as small as 2.5 ac (1 ha) and as large as 4,915 ac (1,989 ha) (Pearl and Hayes 2004, p. 11). Oregon spotted frogs have been found at elevations ranging from near sea level in the Puget Trough lowlands in Washington to approximately 5,000 feet (ft) (1,500 meters (m)) in the Oregon Cascades in western Oregon (Dunlap 1955, p. 316; Hayes 1997, p. 16; McAllister and Leonard 1997, pp. 8-10).

Oregon spotted frogs can make use of a variety of pond types as long as there is sufficient vegetation and seasonal habitat available for egg-laying, tadpole rearing, summer feeding, and overwintering (Pearl et. al. 2009a, p. 144). Oregon spotted frogs at Dempsey Creek in Washington selected areas of relatively shallow water with less emergent vegetation but more submergent vegetation than adjacent habitats. They avoided dry, upland areas of pasture grass (Watson et al. 1998, p. 10; 2000, pp. 54-57; 2003, p. 297). Radio telemetry data indicate Oregon spotted frogs at Dempsey Creek also make extensive use of scrub-shrub wetland habitats adjacent to forested uplands during the winter (moving between the creek and egg-laying areas) (Risenhoover et al. 2001a, p. 13).

Oregon spotted frogs breed in shallow pools (≤14 in (35 cm) deep) that are near flowing water, or which are connected to larger bodies of water during seasonally high water or at flood stage. Characteristic vegetation includes grasses, sedges, and rushes, although eggs are laid where the vegetation is low or sparse, such that vegetation structure does not shade the eggs (McAllister and Leonard 1997, p. 17). While native vegetation is the preferred substrate, the frog also uses short, manipulated, reed canarygrass/native vegetation mix (Engler 1999, pers. comm.). Full solar exposure seems to be a significant factor in egg-laying habitat selection (McAllister and White 2001, p. 12; Pearl and Hayes 2004, p. 18). The availability of the unique characteristics of traditional egg-laying sites is limited, and adults may have limited flexibility to switch sites (Hayes 1994, p. 19). This may make the Oregon spotted frog particularly vulnerable to modification of egg-laying sites (Hayes 1994, p. 19).

After breeding, during the dry season, Oregon spotted frogs move to deeper, permanent pools or creeks (Watson et al. 2003, p. 295). They are often observed near the water's surface basking and feeding in beds of floating and submerged vegetation (Watson et al. 2003, pp. 292-298; Pearl et al. 2005a, pp. 36-37).

Known overwintering sites are associated with flowing systems, such as springs and creeks, that provide well-oxygenated water (Hallock and Pearson 2001, p. 15; Hayes et al. 2001, pp. 20-23; Tattersall and Ultsch 2008, pp. 123, 129, 136) and sheltering locations protected from predators and freezing (Risenhoover et al. 2001b; Watson et al. 2003, p. 295). Oregon spotted frogs apparently burrow in mud, silty substrate; clumps of emergent vegetation; woody accumulations within the creek; and holes in creek banks when inactive during periods of prolonged or severe cold (Watson et al. 2003, p. 295; Hallock and Pearson 2001, p. 16; McAllister and Leonard 1997, p. 17). They are, however, intolerant of anoxic (absence of dissolved oxygen) conditions and are unlikely to burrow into the mud for more than a day or two (Tattersall and Ultsch 2008, p. 136) because survival under anoxic conditions is only a matter of 4 to 7 days (Tattersall and Ultsch 2008, p. 126). This species remains active during the winter and selects microhabitats that can support aerobic metabolism and minimize exposure to predators (Hallock and Pearson 2001, p. 15; Hayes et al. 2001, pp. 20-23; Tattersall and Ultsch 2008, p. 136). In central Oregon, where winters generally result in ice cover over ponds, Oregon spotted frogs follow a fairly reliable routine of considerable activity and movement beneath the ice during the first month following freeze-up. Little movement is observed under the ice in January and February, but activity steadily increases in mid-March, even when ice cover persists (Bowerman 2006, pers. comm.). Radio-tracked frogs remained active all winter, even under the ice at Trout Lake NAP (Hallock and Pearson 2001, pp. 12, 14, 15) and Conboy Lake National Wildlife Refuge (NWR) (Hayes et al. 2001, pp. 16-19).

Results of a habitat utilization and movement study at Dempsey Creek in Washington indicate that adult frogs made infrequent movements between widely separated pools and more frequent movements between pools in closer proximity (Watson et al. 2003, p. 294), but remained within the study area throughout the year. Home ranges averaged 5.4 ac (2.2 ha), and daily movement was 16-23 ft (5-7 m) throughout the year (Watson et al. 2003, p. 295). During the breeding season (February-May), frogs used about half the area used during the rest of the year. During the dry season (June-August), frogs moved to deeper, permanent pools, and occupied the smallest range of any season, then moved back toward their former breeding range during the wet season (September-January) (Watson et al. 2003, p. 295). Individuals equipped with radio transmitters stayed within 2,600 ft (800 m) of capture locations at the Dempsey Creek site (Watson et al. 1998, p. 10) and within about 1,312 ft (400 m) at the Trout Lake NAP (Hallock and Pearson 2001, p. 16).

Recaptures of Oregon spotted frogs at breeding locations in the Buck Lake population in Oregon indicated that adults often move less than 300 ft (100 m) between years (Hayes 1998a, p. 9). However, longer travel distances, while infrequent, have been observed between years and within a single year between seasons. Three adult Oregon spotted frogs (one male and two females) marked in a study at Dempsey Creek and the Black River in Washington moved a distance of 1.5 mi (2.4 km) between seasons along lower Dempsey Creek to the creek's mouth from the point where they were marked (McAllister and Walker 2003, p. 6). An adult female Oregon spotted frog traveled 1,434 ft (437 m) between seasons from its original capture location at the Trout Lake Wetland NAP (Hallock and Pearson 2001, p. 8). Two juvenile frogs at the Jack Creek site in Oregon were recaptured the next summer 4,084 ft (1,245 m) and 4,511 ft (1,375 m) downstream from where they were initially marked, and one adult female moved 9,183 ft (2,799 m) downstream (Cushman and Pearl 2007, p. 13). Oregon spotted frogs at the Sunriver site routinely make annual migrations of 1,640 to 4,265 ft (500 to 1,300 m) between the major breeding complex and an overwintering site (Bowerman 2006, pers. comm.).

While these movement studies are specific to Oregon spotted frogs, the number of studies and size of the study areas are limited and have not been conducted over multiple seasons or years. In addition, the ability to detect frogs is challenging because of the difficult terrain and the need for the receiver and transmitter to be in close proximity. Hammerson (2005) recommends that a 3.1-mile (5-km) dispersal distance be applied to all ranid frog species, because the movement data for ranids are consistent. The preponderance of data indicates that a separation distance of several kilometers may be appropriate and practical for delineation of occupancy, despite occasional movements that are longer or that may allow some genetic interchange between distant populations (for example, the 6.2-mi (10-km) distance noted by Blouin et al. 2010, pp. 2186, 2188). Accordingly, based on the best available scientific information, we presume that Oregon spotted frog habitats are connected for purposes of genetic exchange when occupied/suitable habitats fall within a maximum movement distance of 3.1 mi (5 km).

Historical Range/Distribution

Historically, the Oregon spotted frog ranged from British Columbia to the Pit River basin in northeastern California (Hayes 1997, p. 40; McAllister and Leonard 1997, p. 7). Oregon spotted frogs have been documented at 61 historical localities in 48 watersheds (3 in British Columbia, 13 in Washington, 29 in Oregon, and 3 in California) in 31 sub-basins (McAllister et al. 1993, pp. 11-12; Hayes 1997, p. 41; McAllister and Leonard 1997, pp. 18-20; COSEWIC 2011, pp. 12-13) (see Table 1). We are assuming the watersheds that have recently been documented to be occupied were also occupied historically based on their complete disconnect from known-occupied watersheds and the limited dispersal ability of the Oregon spotted frog. In our analysis of the status and threats to the Oregon spotted frog, we first assessed conditions by breeding location and occupied watersheds, and then summarized the conditions by occupied sub-basin (see Summary of Factors Affecting the Species for more information). Our Threats Synthesis Rangewide Analysis, which includes this finer scale analysis of distribution, is available at http://www.regulations.gov and http://www.fws.gov/wafwo. However, for the rest of the document, we will describe historical and current range or distribution based on river sub-basins/watersheds. A river sub-basin is equivalent to a 4th field watershed and a hydrologic unit code (HUC) of 8. A watershed is equivalent to a 5th field watershed and a HUC 10.

Table 1—Oregon Spotted Frog Historical and Extant Distribution Throughout Range
Location	Sub-basins*: Watersheds
British Columbia	• Lower Fraser River sub-basin near Sumas Prairie in Abbotsford, Nicomen Island in Matsqui, and in Langley Township. Recently (1996/1997 and 2008) discovered at MD Aldergrove, Maria Slough, Mountain Slough, and Morris Valley
Washington Counties: Clark, King, Klickitat, Pierce, Skagit, Snohomish, Thurston, and Whatcom	• Fraser River sub-basin: Recently discovered (2012) in the Sumas River, a tributary to the Lower Chilliwack River watershed;• Nooksack River sub-basin: South Fork Nooksack River (recently discovered (2011 and 2012) in the Black Slough);• Straits of Georgia sub-basin: Recently discovered (2011 and 2012) along the mainstem of the Samish River;
	• Lower Skagit River sub-basin: Skagit River-Frontal Skagit Bay and Finney Creek-Skagit River;
	• Skykomish River sub-basin: Woods Creek-Skykomish River at Monroe;
	• Duwamish River sub-basin: Lower Green River at Kent;
	• Lake Washington sub-basin: Lake Washington at Seattle;
	• Puget Sound (no sub-basin): Chambers Creek-Frontal Puget Sound (Spanaway Lake) and McLane Creek-Frontal Puget Sound (Patterson/Pattison Lake);
	• Nisqually River sub-basin: Lower Nisqually River-Frontal Puget Sound (Kapowsin);

	• Upper Chehalis River sub-basin: Black River (Dempsey Creek, Beaver Creek, Blooms Ditch, and recently discovered in Salmon and Fish Pond Creeks);
	• Lower Willamette River sub-basin: Salmon Creek-Frontal Columbia River at Brush Prairie, Vancouver, and possibly Burnt Bridge Creek at Orchards;
	• Middle Columbia-Hood River sub-basin: White Salmon River (Trout Lake Creek at Gular and Trout Lake);
	• Klickitat River sub-basin: Middle Klickitat River (Conboy Lake on Outlet, Frazier, and Chapman Creeks)
Oregon Counties: Multnomah, Clackamas, Marion, Linn, Benton, Jackson, Lane, Wasco, Deschutes, and Klamath	• Lower Willamette River sub-basin: Johnson Creek;• Lower Deschutes River sub-basin: Tygh Creek and White River;• Clackamas River sub-basin: Oak Grove Fork Clackamas River;• Middle Willamette River sub-basin: Mill Creek-Willamette River and Oak Creek;• South Santiam River sub-basin: South Santiam River-Hamilton Creek;
	• Upper Willamette River sub-basin: Muddy Creek;
	• McKenzie River sub-basin: Upper McKenzie River and South Fork McKenzie River;
	• Middle Fork Willamette River sub-basin: Salt Creek-Willamette River;
	• Upper Deschutes River sub-basin: Deschutes River-McKenzie Canyon, Deschutes River-Pilot Butte, Deschutes River-Fall River, and Deschutes River-Browns Creek;
	• Little Deschutes River sub-basin: Upper Little Deschutes River, Middle Little Deschutes River, Lower Little Deschutes River, Long Prairie, and Crescent Creek;
	• Williamson River sub-basin: Klamath Marsh-Jack Creek, West of Klamath Marsh, and Williamson River above Klamath Marsh
	• Sprague River sub-basin: North Fork Sprague River and Sprague River above Williamson;
	• Upper Klamath Lake sub-basin: Wood River and Klamath Lake watersheds;
	• Upper Klamath sub-basin: Spencer Creek and Jenny Creek;
	• Lost River sub-basin: Lake Ewauna-Upper Klamath River
California Counties: Modoc, Shasta, and Siskiyou	• Lost River sub-basin: Lower Klamath Lake• Upper Pit River sub-basin: Pine Creek-South Pit River (near Alturas)• Lower Pit River sub-basin: Town of Pittville-Pit River (near Fall River Mills)

Current Range/Distribution

Currently, the Oregon spotted frog is found from extreme southwestern British Columbia south through the Puget Trough and in the Cascades Range from south-central Washington at least to the Klamath Basin in southern Oregon. Oregon spotted frogs occur in lower elevations in British Columbia and Washington and are restricted to high elevations in Oregon (Pearl et al. 2010, p. 7). In addition, Oregon spotted frogs currently have a very limited distribution west of the Cascade crest in Oregon, are considered to be extirpated from the Willamette Valley in Oregon (Cushman et al. 2007, p. 14), and may be extirpated in the Klamath and Pit River basins of California (Hayes 1997, p. 1). Currently occupied, or extant, sub-basins are those in which Oregon spotted frogs have been found in since 2000.

In British Columbia, Oregon spotted frogs no longer occupy the locations documented historically, but they currently are known to occupy four disjunct locations in a single sub-basin, the Lower Fraser River (Canadian Oregon Spotted Frog Recovery Team 2012, p. 6).

In Washington, Oregon spotted frogs are known to occur only within six sub-basins/watersheds: The Sumas River, a tributary to the Lower Chilliwack River watershed and Fraser River sub-basin; the Black Slough in the lower South Fork Nooksack River, a tributary of the Nooksack River; Samish River; Black River, a tributary of the Chehalis River; Outlet Creek (Conboy Lake), a tributary to the Middle Klickitat River; and Trout Lake Creek, a tributary of the White Salmon River. The Klickitat and White Salmon Rivers are tributaries to the Columbia River. The Oregon spotted frogs in each of these sub-basins/watersheds are isolated from frogs in other sub-basins.

A reintroduction project was initiated in 2008, at Dailman Lake in Pierce County on Joint Base Lewis-McChord Military Reservation. This sub-basin (Nisqually River) was historically occupied by Oregon spotted frogs with a documented occurrence at Kapowsin (McAllister and Leonard 1997, pp. 18-19). Eggs were collected from the Black River and the Conboy Lake Oregon spotted frog egg-laying locations, captive reared until metamorphosis, and released in the fall or subsequent spring. Through 2011, researchers collected 7,870 eggs and released 3,355 frogs (Tirhi and Schmidt 2011, pp. 51-53). Surveys in April 2011 found 3 verified Oregon spotted frog egg masses and 11 suspected egg masses. However, egg masses were not detected in 2012. This effort is ongoing, and the efficacy and viability of a breeding Oregon spotted frog population being established in this area is undetermined; therefore, this location will not be discussed further. However, should a population be established, it would be considered to be a part of the listed entity.

In Oregon, Oregon spotted frogs are known to occur only within eight sub-basins: Lower Deschutes River, Upper Deschutes River, Little Deschutes River, McKenzie River, Middle Fork Willamette, Upper Klamath, Upper Klamath Lake, and the Williamson River. The Oregon spotted frogs in most of these sub-basins are isolated from frogs in other sub-basins, although Oregon spotted frogs in the lower Little Deschutes River are aquatically connected with those below Wickiup Reservoir in the Upper Deschutes River sub-basin. Oregon spotted frog distribution west of the Cascade Mountains in Oregon is restricted to a few lakes in the upper watersheds of the McKenzie River and Middle Fork Willamette River sub-basins, which represent the remaining 2 out of 12 historically occupied sub-basins.

In California, this species has not been detected since 1918 (California Academy of Science Museum Record 44291) at historical sites and may be extirpated (Hayes 1997, pp. 1, 35). However, there has been limited survey effort of potential habitat and this species may still occur in California.

Population Estimates and Status

Of the 61 historical localities where the species' previous existence can be verified (e. g., museum specimens, photographs, reliable published records), only 13 were confirmed as being occupied in studies conducted in the 1990s (Hayes 1997, p. 1; McAllister and Leonard 1997, p. 20). Hayes visited historical localities one to four times, with a minimum of 2 hours devoted to site visits where precise localities could be identified. For sites where the precise location was not known, he searched three to six points in the area that possessed favorable habitat, for 20 minutes to 3 hours, depending on site size. Hayes also visited sites that were judged to have a high likelihood of having Oregon spotted frogs (i.e., within the historical range, consistent with elevations documented for verifiable specimens, and within suitable habitat) (Hayes 1997, p. 6). Based on those studies, Hayes (1997, p. 1) estimated the species may no longer occur in 76 to 90 percent of its historical range. Although this estimated loss of historical localities did not account for potential range expansion or shifts, Oregon spotted frogs have not been subsequently relocated in these areas. The estimated loss in historical range does not take into account the localities found since 2000. However, the current range of the Oregon spotted frog is significantly smaller than the historical range, based on the best available scientific and commercial information.

Egg mass counts are believed to be a good metric of adult population size and are the most time-efficient way to estimate population size (Phillipsen et al. 2010, p. 743). Adult females are believed to lay one egg mass per year (Phillipsen et al. 2010, p. 743), and the breeding period occurs within a reliable and predictable timeframe each year (McAllister 2006, pers. comm.). If egg mass numbers are collected in a single survey timed to coincide with the end of the breeding season, when egg laying should be complete, then the egg mass count should represent a reliable estimate of total egg masses. Because one egg mass is approximately equivalent to one breeding female plus one to two adult males, a rough estimate of adult population size can be made if a thorough egg mass census is completed (Phillipsen et al. 2010, p. 743). However, using egg mass counts to estimate population size has some weaknesses. For example, researchers have uncertainties about whether adult females breed every year, only lay one egg mass per year, and find difficulty in distinguishing individual egg masses in large communal clusters. However, a minimum population estimate can be derived from the total egg mass count multiplied by two (one egg mass equals two adult frogs). While there are weaknesses in these estimates, as discussed above, they are the best estimates available for Oregon spotted frog numbers.

Egg mass counts, as currently conducted at most sites, do not allow for evaluation of trends within a site nor between sites because surveys are not standardized. Survey effort, area coverage, and timing can differ between years at individual sites. In addition, method of survey can differ between years at individual sites and differ between sites. Because of the weaknesses associated with the egg mass counts, site estimates derived from egg mass counts are considered to be a minimum estimate and generally should not be compared across years or with other sites. However, some breeding locations have been surveyed in a consistent manner (in some cases by the same researcher) and for enough years that trend data are available and considered to be reliable. Trend information is provided in the following sub-basin summaries for the locations where the information is available.

For the purposes of this document, the terms 'location' and 'site' simply refer to the general locations where egg-laying has been observed. In some cases, a site may be equivalent to an Oregon spotted frog population (for example, Hosmer Lake). In other cases, a site may include multiple egg-laying locations within wetland complexes where hydrological connections may facilitate movement between egg-laying areas, but where movement patterns and genetic conditions are undetermined within the complexes (for example, Klamath Marsh NWR). Accordingly, a site should not be interpreted to be a population. Because of the lack of complete information between occurrence locations, populations were not specifically identified for this status review, and the focus of our analysis regarding the status of Oregon spotted frogs was within the individual river sub-basins.

The following summarizes the best available scientific and commercial information available regarding populations within the currently occupied river sub-basins in British Columbia, Washington, and Oregon. We used multiple data sources, including various unpublished reports, databases, and spreadsheets provided by our partner agencies. These sources are identified in the following sections as "multiple data sources" and are included in our literature cited list, which is included as supplementary information on http://www.regulations.gov for this final rule. These sources are available upon request from the Washington Fish and Wildlife Office (see ADDRESSES). In most sub-basins, trend information regarding the collective status of the populations within the sub-basin is limited or not available; trend information that was available is presented below. The status of a sub-basin may be undetermined because the Oregon spotted frog presence has only recently been identified, the trend information is uncertain, or sufficient survey information is not available to indicate a trend. However, when viewed at the rangewide scale, the Oregon spotted frog has been extirpated from most of its historical range, and the threat of current and future impacts to the Oregon spotted frog occurs over the entire range of the species. Ongoing threats have significantly reduced the overall extent and distribution of suitable habitat for the Oregon spotted frog, as discussed below in Summary of Factors Affecting the Species.

British Columbia

Currently, Oregon spotted frogs are known to occur only within four sites in the Lower Fraser River Basin. Of the four sites, Maintenance Detachment Aldergrove (MD Aldergrove) is nearing, or may have reached extirpation, as no egg masses have been discovered at the site since 2006; Mountain Slough appears to be stable; Maria Slough may be declining; and there are limited data for the recently discovered Morris Valley site (COSEWIC 2011, p. v). Estimates from the well-studied populations at MD Aldergrove, Maria Slough, and Mountain Slough indicate a population decline of 35 percent during the period 2000-2010 (COSEWIC 2011, p. 32), and the most recent egg mass counts indicate the minimum population size for all of British Columbia is fewer than 350 adults (COSEWIC 2011, pp. 27-30). One extant population is near extinction, and the remaining populations are small and vulnerable to disturbance and stochastic events. Extirpation of the MD Aldergrove population would result in a reduction of 76 percent of the extent of Oregon spotted frog in the Lower Fraser River (COSEWIC 2011, pp. vii-ix). Therefore, populations of Oregon spotted frogs in the Lower Fraser River are declining.

Washington

In Washington, the Oregon spotted frog was historically found in the Puget Trough from the Canadian border to the Columbia River, and east to the Washington Cascades (McAllister et al. 1997, p. vii). Current distribution is limited to four watersheds in the Puget Trough, three that drain to Puget Sound and one that drains to the Pacific Ocean, and two watersheds in the southeast Cascades that drain to the Columbia River. In 1997, the locations for 11 historical populations in Washington were verified using museum specimen and published records, and only 1 historically known population and 2 recently discovered populations were known to remain in Washington in 1997 (McAllister et al. 1997, p. vii). The authors also stated that past populations of the Oregon spotted frog in Washington are largely undocumented (McAllister et al. 1997, p. 18). Current population estimates are based on the 2012 census of egg masses at all known extant breeding areas. Based on these estimates, the minimum population in Washington was at least 7,368 breeding adults in 2012.

Trend data are limited; however, the Oregon spotted frog population in the Middle Klickitat River (Conboy Lake) appears to be declining (see below for further information). The population trend within the rest of the occupied sub-basins is unknown. More detailed discussions of Washington's occupied sub-basins/watersheds are provided below.

Lower Chilliwack River (Sumas River)— In 2012, one Oregon spotted frog breeding area was found on a privately owned dairy farm on a small tributary to the Sumas River (Bohannon et al. 2012). The Sumas River is eventually a tributary to the Lower Fraser River, along which the British Columbia breeding areas occur. However, the breeding area on the Sumas River is more than 20 mi (35 km) upstream of the confluence with the Fraser River, and separated by unsuitable aquatic habitat. Therefore, an aquatic connection to the British Columbia breeding areas is not likely (COSEWIC 2011, p. 12). Fewer than 50 egg masses (<100 adults) were found during the 2012 surveys; however, suitable habitat within the Sumas River has not been surveyed extensively (Bohannon et al. 2012) and the full extent of Oregon spotted frog distribution and abundance has not been determined.

South Fork Nooksack River— In 2011 and 2012, Oregon spotted frog breeding areas were found on privately owned parcels in the Black Slough, a tributary of the South Fork Nooksack River. On one parcel, the breeding habitat was in off-channel wetlands dominated by reed canarygrass (Phalaris arundinacea) and recent shrub plantings. Breeding areas on other parcels were located within former pasture lands that had been planted with trees and fenced within the last 2 or 3 years under the Conservation Reserve Enhancement Program (CREP) to eliminate grazing and improve water quality (Bohannon et al. 2012). At least 230 adults (based on 2012 surveys) are associated with the known breeding areas along the Black Slough; however, this area has not been surveyed extensively (Bohannon et al. 2012), and the full extent of Oregon spotted frog distribution and abundance has not been determined.

Samish River— In 2011 and 2012, Oregon spotted frog breeding areas were found on privately owned parcels along the upper reaches of the Samish River. All of the breeding areas are seasonally flooded grazed or formerly grazed pasture lands that are predominantly reed canarygrass (Bohannon et al. 2012). At least 1,220 adults (based on 2012 surveys) are associated with the known breeding areas along the Samish River; however, this area has not been surveyed extensively, and the full extent of Oregon spotted frog distribution and abundance has not been determined.

Black River— Oregon spotted frogs occupy wetlands in the floodplain and tributaries of the upper Black River drainage between Black Lake and the town of Littlerock. They are currently known to occur at three locations within the Black River floodplain (Blooms Ditch near 110th Avenue Bridge, near 123rd Avenue, and the confluence with Mima Creek) and in four tributaries: Dempsey Creek, Salmon Creek, Allen Creek, and Beaver Creek (Hallock 2013; WDFW and USFWS multiple data sources). In 2012 and 2013, new breeding locations were detected along Fish Pond Creek system, which flows directly into Black Lake, not Black River. Oregon spotted frog breeding areas in the Black River may be isolated from each other and the frogs associated with the Fish Pond Creek may not be hydrologically connected to frogs in the Black River due to the human alteration of the Black Lake drainage pattern. Further investigation of this recently discovered area is needed.

The full extent of the population's distribution, abundance, and status in the Black River has not been determined. The Black River adult breeding population was comprised of at least 1,748 breeding adults in 2012 (Hallock 2013, p. 27) and 3,330 breeding adults in 2013 (WDFW multiple data sources). Oregon spotted frogs in Dempsey Creek have been monitored relatively consistently since the late 1990s. Other breeding areas in the Black River have been monitored inconsistently or were recently found, and surveys to identify additional breeding locations continue. The Dempsey Creek breeding area may be declining, but the trend for the remainder of the occupied areas is undetermined.

White Salmon River (Trout Lake Creek) — Oregon spotted frogs occupy approximately 1,285 ac (520 ha) of the lower Trout Lake Creek watershed, ranging in elevation 1,960-2,080 ft (597-633 m). In total, as of 2012, a minimum population estimate of 2,124 breeding adults (Hallock 2012) associated with 12 breeding areas have been identified. Two of the breeding areas have been monitored since they were found by Leonard (1997). The other locations have been monitored sporadically since they were discovered. Monitoring of egg mass numbers at two breeding areas within the Trout Lake NAP revealed considerable population volatility and a general pattern of decline from 2001 through 2007 (Hallock 2011, p. 8). During the period of egg mass declines, three events of note occurred that could have influenced frogs at the NAP: Annual precipitation was unusually low, cattle grazing was reduced and then eliminated, and frogs infected with chytrid fungus (Batrachochytrium dendrobatidis (Bd)) were present (Pearl et al. 2009b, Hayes et al. 2009). While the 2009 through 2012 egg mass counts indicate that Oregon spotted frog numbers may be rebounding within the eastern portions of the NAP, the numbers in the western portion continue to be less than half of the estimates from the 1990s (Hallock 2012, entire).

Middle Klickitat River (Conboy Lake) — The extent of Conboy Lake wetland complex habitat occupied by Oregon spotted frogs at high water is approximately 7,462 ac (3,020 ha), ranging in elevation from 1,804-1,896 ft (550-576 m). This wetland complex comprises two lakebeds that are entirely seasonal (except in wet years) and are joined by Camas Ditch, which flows into Outlet Creek, the main drainage for the system that flows northeast into the Klickitat River. There were a minimum of 1,954 breeding adults in the Conboy Lake wetland complex in 2012 (Hallock 2013, p. 27) and 2,714 breeding adults in 2013 (Wilson, in lit. 2013). This used to be the largest Oregon spotted frog population throughout the entire range (highest egg mass count 7,018 in year 1998). However, Oregon spotted frog egg mass surveys suggest a continued long-term decline (approximately 86 percent) since 1998 (Hayes and Hicks 2011, unnumbered pp. 5-6; Hallock 2013, p. 36). This area is subject to similar levels of precipitation as Trout Lake NAP and frogs infected with Bd were also present (Pearl et al. 2009b, Hayes et al. 2009); however, unlike Trout Lake NAP, Oregon spotted frog numbers in this sub-basin are not rebounding. At present, the population trend of Oregon spotted frogs in the Middle Klickitat River is considered to be declining.

Oregon

Population estimates of Oregon spotted frogs in Oregon are primarily based on egg mass surveys conducted in 2011 and 2012 at known extant sites, and newly discovered occupied areas that had been unsurveyed prior to 2012. Population estimates for the Middle Fork Willamette River sub-basin are based on mark-recapture studies conducted by U.S. Geological Survey (USGS) in 2011, rather than egg mass surveys. Based on these survey data, the minimum population estimate in Oregon consists of approximately 12,847 breeding adults. More detailed discussions of Oregon's occupied sub-basins are provided below and are available in our files.

Lower Deschutes River— Within the Lower Deschutes River sub-basin, a single extant population of Oregon spotted frog occurs at Camas Prairie, an 82-ac (33-ha) marsh located along Camas Creek in the White River watershed. The Camas Prairie Oregon spotted frogs are the most geographically isolated, carry several alleles that are absent or rare in other sites, and have the lowest genetic diversity of Oregon spotted frogs rangewide (Blouin et al. 2010, p. 2185). The frogs at this location appear to be the only remaining representatives of a major genetic group that is now almost extinct (Blouin et al. 2010, p. 2190). Since 2004, egg mass surveys have been conducted annually, and the population trend has been positive. Based on the 2012 egg mass count, the minimum population size of breeding adults is 152 (Corkran 2012, pers. comm.). Although the population trend has been positive at the single known location, the number of individuals in the population remains low.

Upper Deschutes River— Oregon spotted frogs in the Upper Deschutes River sub-basin occur in high-elevation lakes up to 5,000 ft (1,524 m), wetland ponds, and riverine wetlands and oxbows along the Deschutes River. There are fewer than 20 known breeding locations within four watersheds (HUC 10) in the sub-basin: Charleton Creek, Browns Creek, Fall River, and North Unit Diversion Dam. Most of the known breeding locations are on the Deschutes National Forest in lakes, ponds, and riverine wetlands that drain to the Crane Prairie and Wickiup Reservoir complex, including the use of the wetland margins of the reservoirs. There are at least five known breeding locations downstream of Wickiup Reservoir in riverine wetlands along the Deschutes River, extending to Bend, Oregon: Dead Slough, La Pine SP, Sunriver, Slough Camp, and the Old Mill casting pond, including Les Schwab Amphitheater (LSA) Marsh. Dilman Meadow drains into the Deschutes River below Wickiup Dam via an unnamed tributary.

The consistency of population surveys varies by breeding site, and population trend information is limited. Only two sites within the sub-basin have been monitored consistently since the early 2000s and show an increasing population trend: Dilman Meadow and Sunriver (USGS and J. Bowerman 2000 through 2012 datasets). Trend data are not available for the remainder of populations within the Upper Deschutes River sub-basin. Sunriver, located downstream of Wickiup Reservoir, is the largest population of Oregon spotted frogs within the Upper Deschutes River sub-basin with a population of at least 1,454 breeding adults based on 2012 egg mass surveys (J. Bowerman dataset 2012). A minimum population estimate for the Upper Deschutes River sub-basin (including Sunriver) is approximately 3,530 breeding adults based on surveys since 2006 (USGS 2006 to 2012 and J. Bowerman 2012 datasets).

Little Deschutes River— Oregon spotted frogs are distributed throughout wetland, pond, and riverine habitats in the Little Deschutes River sub-basin, which drains an area of approximately 1,020 square miles (2,600 square km) and flows north from its headwaters in northern Klamath County to its convergence with the Deschutes River 1 mi (1.2 km) south of Sunriver and approximately 20 mi (32 km) south of Bend, Oregon. The Little Deschutes River is approximately 92 mi (148 km) long. Approximately 23 known breeding locations (as of 2012) are within five watersheds in the sub-basin: Upper, Middle, and Lower Little Deschutes River; Crescent Creek; and Long Prairie. Big Marsh, a 2,000-ac (809 ha) wetland located within headwaters at 4,760 ft (1,451 m) elevation on the Deschutes National Forest, has the largest monitored population of Oregon spotted frogs in the Little Deschutes River sub-basin and possibly rangewide. The estimated population size of Big Marsh based on a 2012 U.S. Forest Service (USFS) egg mass survey is 5,324 breeding adults (male and female) (USFS data 2012).

Because 70 percent of the sub-basin is privately owned and mostly unsurveyed, a population estimate for the entire Little Deschutes River sub-basin is difficult to determine. A minimum population estimate of Oregon spotted frogs based on limited survey data from public and private lands in 2012 is approximately 6,628 breeding adults (including Big Marsh above). However, the vast acreage of wetland complexes and suitable habitat for Oregon spotted frogs along the mainstem Little Deschutes River and Crescent Creek indicate that the frog population within the unsurveyed areas may be well above this estimate. Although the trend of the frog population at Big Marsh appears to be increasing based on USFS surveys from 2002 to 2012 (USFS 2002-2012), the population trend of the remainder of frogs within the sub-basin is undetermined.

McKenzie River— Oregon spotted frogs in the McKenzie River sub-basin are located within the South Fork McKenzie River watershed in an area referred to as the Mink Lake Basin in the wilderness of the Willamette National Forest. There are two known breeding populations: One at Penn Lake and one at an unnamed marsh 0.28 mi (0.45 km) north of Mink Lake. The Penn Lake and Unnamed Marsh populations are about 0.93 mi (1.5 km) apart and are not hydrologically connected via surface water. Mark-recapture monitoring of these populations has been conducted by USGS from 2007 through 2011 (Adams et al. 2007; 2008, p. 13; 2009, p. 14; 2010, p. 14; and 2011, p. 14). A population estimate for breeding adults in the McKenzie River sub-basin, based on mark-recapture efforts by USGS in 2011 is 217 (i.e., 179 at Penn Lake and 38 at Unnamed Marsh) (Adams et al. 2011). However, trend has not been estimated for these populations.

Middle Fork Willamette River— Oregon spotted frogs in the Middle Fork Willamette River sub-basin are limited to a single population at Gold Lake and bog, located in the 465-ac (188-ha) Gold Lake Bog Research Natural Area on the Willamette National Forest within the Salt Creek watershed. This population is one of three remaining populations of Oregon spotted frogs west of the Cascade mountain crest in Oregon. The Gold Lake Bog site consists of three small ponds over an area of approximately 3.7 ac (1.5 ha) within a larger bog where three major streams converge. Breeding surveys are periodically conducted by USGS and the Willamette National Forest. However, long-term trend data are lacking for this site. Based on USGS egg mass surveys in 2007, the estimated population size is approximately 1,458 breeding adults (USGS datasets).

Williamson River— Oregon spotted frogs in the Williamson River sub-basin occur in two watersheds: Klamath Marsh/Jack Creek and Williamson River above Klamath Marsh and consist of three populations: Jack Creek, Klamath Marsh NWR, and the Upper Williamson River. Data from 1996 through the present suggest the Jack Creek population is declining, and the survey data from 2000 through the present suggest that the Klamath Marsh population is stable. Additional data collected in 2013 documented a downstream extension of occupied habitat in Jack Creek (Pearl 2014, pers. comm.). These watersheds are a mixture of both private and public (U.S. Bureau of Land Management (BLM), USFS, and NWR) lands and consist of both wetland and riverine potential habitats from 4,500 to 5,200 ft (1,371 to 1,585 m) in elevation. As of 2011, the minimum population estimate for the sub-basin is approximately 376 breeding individuals (male and female) (KMNWR 2011, USFS 2012, USGS multiple datasets). Permission to survey adjacent private lands has not been obtained; however, the private lands surrounding the public lands appear to have suitable habitat and likely contain additional breeding complexes and individuals.

Upper Klamath Lake— Oregon spotted frogs in the Upper Klamath Lake sub-basin occupy two watersheds that flow into Upper Klamath Lake: Klamath Lake and Wood River. There are four populations in this sub-basin: Crane Creek, Fourmile Creek, Sevenmile Creek, and the Wood River channel and the adjacent but separate BLM Wood River canal. Additional surveys completed in 2013 revealed occupied habitat in Sun Creek, Annie Creek, and more locations of Crane Creek and Sevenmile Creek (Hering 2014, pers. comm.; Pearl 2013, pers. comm.). These populations occur in both riverine and wetland habitats. Historically, these two watersheds were hydrologically connected. Survey efforts on Fourmile Creek, Sevenmile Creek, and the Wood River channel have been sporadic while Crane Creek and the BLM Wood River canal have been surveyed annually. These data suggest that there is still insufficient information to obtain population trends for all but the BLM Wood River canal population, which is declining. As of 2011, the minimum population estimate for the sub-basin is approximately 374 breeding individuals (male and female) (USGS multiple datasets, BLM multiple datasets). Permission to survey adjacent private lands has not been obtained; however, the private lands surrounding the known populations appear to have suitable habitat and likely contain additional breeding complexes and individuals. Trend data are lacking for three out of four populations in the Upper Klamath Lake.

Upper Klamath— Oregon spotted frogs in the Upper Klamath sub-basin occupy two lacustrine habitats: Parsnip Lakes in Jackson County and Buck Lake in Klamath County. Both of these sites are isolated hydrologically by great distances (>20 mi (32 km)) and hydrological barriers (inhospitable habitat and dams) to other sites in the Klamath Basin. Historical surveys in this sub-basin resulted in a population estimate of about 1,170 adults (range of <0 to 2,379, 95 percent confidence interval) (Hayes 1998a, p. 10; Parker 2009, p. 4). Due to insufficient survey data, population trend information is not available for the Parsnip Lakes population. The most recent surveys found 18 egg masses or 36 breeding individuals (male and female) at Parsnips Lakes (Parker 2009). Surveys conducted at Buck Lake suggest a population decline and have documented most recently small numbers of egg masses (38 masses in 2010), or the equivalent of 76 breeding individual (male and female) (BLM 2012). Additional information indicates that suitable habitat occurs downstream of Buck Lake within Spencer Creek (Smith 2014, pers. comm.). The minimum population estimate for this sub-basin is currently estimated to be 112 breeding individuals suggesting drastic population declines since 1998.

Summary of Current Population Range and Trend

Oregon spotted frogs may no longer occur in as much as 90 percent of their historically documented range, including all of the historical localities in California (i.e., 90 percent of the historical areas are no longer occupied). Currently, the Oregon spotted frog is found in 15 sub-basins ranging from extreme southwestern British Columbia south through the Puget Trough, and in the Cascades Range from south-central Washington at least to the Klamath Basin in Oregon. Oregon spotted frogs occur in lower elevations in British Columbia and Washington and are restricted to higher elevations (i.e., 3,160 to 5,200 ft (963 to 1,585 m) in Oregon. In addition, Oregon spotted frogs currently have a very limited distribution west of the Cascade crest in Oregon and are considered to be extirpated from the Willamette Valley.

In most sub-basins, trend information regarding the collective status of the populations within the sub-basin is limited or not available. The best scientific and commercial information available indicates the trend is undetermined for Oregon spotted frog populations in 13 of the sub-basins and is declining in the Lower Fraser River and Middle Klickitat sub-basins. Threats to the remaining populations are ongoing or increasing, however, as described below.

Summary of Factors Affecting the Species

Section 4 of the Act (16 U.S.C. 1533), and its implementing regulations at 50 CFR part 424, set forth the procedures for adding species to the Federal Lists of Endangered and Threatened Wildlife and Plants. Under section 4(a)(1) of the Act, we may list a species based on any of the following five factors: (A) The present or threatened destruction, modification, or curtailment of its habitat or range; (B) overutilization for commercial, recreational, scientific, or educational purposes; (C) disease or predation; (D) the inadequacy of existing regulatory mechanisms; and (E) other natural or manmade factors affecting its continued existence. Listing actions may be warranted based on any of the above threat factors, singly or in combination. Each of these threats/factors is discussed below.

Threats for the Oregon spotted frog were assessed by breeding locations and occupied watersheds, then summarized by occupied sub-basin in this final rule. Each of the five threat categories were summarized by sub-basin using the unified threats classification system (loosely based on the IUCN-CMP (World Conservation Union-Conservation Measures Partnership)), best available data, and best professional judgment. We summarized threats in each occupied sub-basin for scope, severity, impact, timing, and stress, to ensure our determination would be based on the best scientific and commercial data available, as required under section 4(b)(1)(A). Scope is the proportion of the occupied area within the sub-basin that can reasonably be expected to be affected. Severity is the level of damage to the species from the threat that can reasonably be expected. Impact summarizes the degree to which a species is observed, inferred, or suspected to be directly or indirectly affected and is based on the combination of the severity and scope rating (for example, if the severity and scope ratings were both high, then the impact rating was high). Timing is the immediacy of the threat (i.e., is the threat ongoing, could happen in the short term, or is only in the past). Stress is the key ecological, demographic, or individual attribute that may be impaired or reduced by a threat. The completed analysis (Threats Synthesis Rangewide Analysis) is available at http://www.regulations.gov and http://www.fws.gov/wafwo. The syntheses by threat categories are included in the following threat factor discussions.

Large historical losses of wetland habitat have occurred across the range of the Oregon spotted frog. Wetland losses are estimated from between 30 to 85 percent across the species' range with the greatest percentage lost having occurred in British Columbia. These wetland losses have directly influenced the current fragmentation and isolation of remaining Oregon spotted frog populations.

Loss of natural wetland and riverine disturbance processes as a result of human activities has and continues to result in degradation of Oregon spotted frog habitat. Historically, a number of disturbance processes created emergent wetlands favorable to Oregon spotted frogs throughout the PNW: (1) Rivers freely meandered over their floodplains, removing trees and shrubs and baring patches of mineral soil; (2) beavers created a complex mosaic of aquatic habitat types for year-round use; and (3) summer fires burned areas that would be shallow water wetlands during the Oregon spotted frog breeding season the following spring. Today, all of these natural processes are greatly reduced, are impaired, or have been permanently altered as a result of human activities, including stream bank, channel, and wetland modifications; operation of water control structures (e.g., dams and diversions); beaver removal; and fire suppression.

The historical loss of Oregon spotted frog habitats and lasting anthropogenic changes in natural disturbance processes are exacerbated by the introduction of reed canarygrass, nonnative predators, and potentially climate change. In addition, current regulatory mechanisms and voluntary incentive programs designed to benefit fish species have inadvertently led to the continuing decline in quality of Oregon spotted frog habitats in some locations. The current wetland and stream vegetation management paradigm is generally a no-management or restoration approach that often results in succession to a tree- and shrub-dominated community that unintentionally degrades or eliminates remaining or potential suitable habitat for Oregon spotted frog breeding. Furthermore, incremental wetland loss or degradation continues under the current regulatory mechanisms. If left unmanaged, these factors are anticipated to result in the eventual elimination of remaining suitable Oregon spotted frog habitats or populations. The persistence of habitats required by the species is now largely management-dependent.

Factor A. The Present or Threatened Destruction, Modification, or Curtailment of Its Habitat or Range

Threats to the species' habitat include changes in hydrology due to construction of dams and human-related alterations to seasonal flooding, introduction of nonnative plant and animal species, vegetation succession and encroachment, poor water quality, livestock grazing (in some circumstances), and residential and commercial development.

Habitat losses and alterations affect amphibian species in a variety of ways, including reducing or eliminating immigration through losses of adjacent populations (see "Factor E") and effects on critical aspects of the habitat (Hayes and Jennings 1986, pp. 492-494). These critical aspects include suitable egg-laying and nursery sites, refuges from predation or unfavorable environmental conditions, and suitable temperatures necessary for egg laying, growth, and development (Hayes and Jennings 1986, pp. 492-494).

Because Oregon spotted frogs have specific habitat requirements, they are particularly vulnerable to habitat alterations: (1) A restricted number of communal egg-laying locations are used year after year; (2) the species' warm water microhabitat requirement results in habitat overlap with introduced warm water fish species and other warm water fauna that prey on Oregon spotted frogs (for example, bullfrogs); (3) the availability of suitable warm water habitat, a requirement in the active season, is generally limited in the cool climate of the PNW; (4) the species is vulnerable to the loss or alteration of springs used for overwintering; and (5) their habitat requirements (for example, spatial structure) for overwintering, active season, and breeding habitats are more complex than for other frog species (Hayes et al. 1997, p. 4). In addition, breeding habitat is arguably the single most important habitat component for many aquatic-breeding amphibians because amphibian embryos and larvae depend on aquatic habitats for survival (Leonard 1997, p.

1).

Loss of Wetlands

British Columbia— Extensive diking of river ways and draining of Sumas Lake for conversion to agriculture significantly modified drainage patterns and resulted in loss of associated wetlands in the Fraser River lowlands of British Columbia (COSEWIC 2011, p. 20). Boyle et al. (1997, p. 190) estimated an 85 percent loss of habitat types preferred by Oregon spotted frogs (fen, swamp/bog/marsh) between 1820 and 1990. Moore et al. (2003 cited in COSEWIC 2011) found wetland loss continued between 1989 and 1999 as a result of urban and agricultural encroachment. Agricultural land use changes, such as the conversion of field habitat to blueberry and cranberry production, has led to impacts through drain tile installation and riparian area encroachment/erosion. Sediment deposition into streams and wetlands by runoff from adjacent agricultural fields can impact Oregon spotted frog breeding habitat by changing the channel/wetland shape and depth (Lynch and Corbett 1990). Land conversion for agriculture is ongoing at Mountain Slough and to some extent at Maria Slough and Morris Valley (COSFRT 2012, p. 24), within Oregon spotted frog habitat.

Washington— Estimates for Washington indicate that over 33 percent of wetlands were drained, diked, and filled between pre-settlement times and the 1980s (Canning and Stevens 1990, p. 23); losses in the historical range of the Oregon spotted frog are even higher because of the high degree of development in the low elevations of the Puget Trough (McAllister and Leonard 1997, p. 22).

Major alterations to Conboy Lake wetland complex in Washington began when settlers started moving to Glenwood Valley in the late 1800s. Wet meadows were drained through a series of canals, ditches, and dikes largely developed between 1911 and 1914, and remain today. The five creeks that flow into this wetland complex and the Cold Springs ditch are entirely channelized within the wetland complex. Ditching, filling, and other habitat alterations have resulted in little or no retention of surface water in the late-season lakebeds (Conboy Lake and Camas Prairie), reducing the amount of aquatic habitat available for the Oregon spotted frog. The historical Conboy lakebed is believed to have retained water for 10 to 12 months in most years. Currently, it retains water only during wet years and is purposefully drained annually to control bullfrogs (Ludwig 2012, pers. comm.). The Camas Prairie portion of Glenwood Valley retains water year-round over a small area and only in wet years. Typically, aquatic habitat is reduced to about 1,000 ac (400 ha) during the late summer and early fall (Hayes et al. 2000), and once the seasonal lakebeds dry, the network of ditches and channels provide the only aquatic habitat for Oregon spotted frogs. In order to maintain sufficient flow through the system, a small area of Bird Creek must be excavated every 2 to 3 years to remove the high level of sand and gravel that is deposited annually from upstream. Most of the other ditches have been cleaned on a much less frequent basis (intervals of up to 20 years), although in the future, the Conboy Lake NWR plans to clean select reaches on a 5-10 year cycle (Ludwig 2012, pers. comm.).

Oregon— Historical losses of wetland in Oregon are estimated at 38 percent between pre-settlement times and the 1980s with 57 and 91 percent of these losses concentrated in the Willamette Valley and Klamath Basin, respectively (Dahl 1990). Wetland loss continues in the Willamette Valley (Daggett et al. 1998; Morlan et al. 2005). Between 1982 and 1994, a net loss of 6,877 ac (2,783 ha) of wetlands (2.5 percent of the 1982 wetland area) occurred, primarily due to conversion to agriculture (Daggett et al. 1998 p. 23), and between 1994 and 2005, an estimated additional net loss of 3,932 ac (1,591 ha) (1.25 percent of the 1994 wetland area) took place, primarily due to development (Morlan et al. 2010. pp. 26-27). Oregon spotted frogs are believed to be extirpated from the Willamette Valley.

Human alteration of wetlands in the central Oregon Cascades has had less severe effects since many of the sites inhabited by the Oregon spotted frog are located at high elevation and within lakes and wetlands located on Federal lands managed by the USFS. However, damming and diverting water for irrigation needs has resulted in the loss of wetlands within the Upper Deschutes sub-basin beginning in the early 1900s (see hydrology section below). Wetland loss is also an ongoing threat to Oregon spotted frogs within the Little Deschutes River sub-basin in south Deschutes County, where land development has increased since the 1960s.

A substantial amount of wetland habitat in the Klamath Basin has been drained and converted to other uses, primarily for grazing and row-crop production, although the extent of this loss is difficult to estimate due to a lack of accurate historical data (Larson and Brush 2010). The majority of wetland degradation and alteration took place in the southern part of the upper basin, where extensive drainage occurred at Tule and Lower Klamath Lakes in the early 20th century (Larson and Brush 2010, p. 4). Wetlands at the north end of the basin, including Sycan Marsh, Klamath Marsh, Upper Klamath Lake, and in the Wood River Valley, have also suffered extensive hydrologic alteration. Ongoing losses are currently minimized due to strict regulations governing wetlands, and there are no known ongoing losses of wetlands in the Klamath Basin. In addition, restoration efforts are under way in the Klamath Basin (see "Conservation Efforts to Reduce Habitat Destruction, Modification, or Curtailment of Its Range"), reversing wetland losses to some degree. However, because of subsidence, reconnection of former wetlands to Upper Klamath Lake resulted in these areas being too deep to support marsh vegetation, and many of these areas do not support the variety of wildlife that they did formerly when they were marshes. Therefore, these wetlands are unlikely to provide all of their former functions.

Loss of Wetlands Conclusion— Historical loss of wetlands has been extensive throughout the range of the species, and is the primary reason for the absence of the species from as much as, or more than, 90 percent of its former range (also see Historical Range/Distribution). Land conversions that result in loss of wetlands are continuing throughout the range. Wetlands continue to be lost or degraded in at least 10 of the 15 occupied sub-basins. Even though these losses are occurring at much lower rates than in the past because of Federal and State regulations that pertain to wetlands (see Factor D), the ongoing loss of wetlands continues to pose a threat to the Oregon spotted frog.

Hydrological Changes

Changing water levels at critical periods in the Oregon spotted frog's life cycle, whether natural or human-induced, has negatively affected the species. Lowered water levels have exposed individuals to predation by reducing cover and confining them to smaller areas where they are more vulnerable to predators (see also Factor C). Water level reduction during the breeding season, due to both natural and anthropogenic causes, has resulted in the loss of the entire reproductive effort for the year due to stranding and desiccation of the egg masses in British Columbia (Licht 1971, p. 122; COSFRT 2012, p. 18), Washington (Lewis et al. 2001, p. 8; Hayes et al. 2000, pp. 6-7), and Oregon (Pearl and Hayes 2004, p. 24). Excessive seasonal flooding at critical periods has also resulted in the loss of shallow wetlands needed for egg-laying and development.

Most of the currently occupied Oregon spotted frog sites face threats from changes in hydrology. Twenty-one of twenty-eight (75 percent) sites surveyed in Washington and Oregon have had some human-related hydrological alterations, ranging from minor changes (for example, local ditching around springs) to substantial changes, including major modifications of historical flow patterns

(Hayes 1997, p. 43; Hayes et al. 1997, p. 6). Oregon spotted frogs in four of the occupied sub-basins (Lower Fraser River, Middle Klickitat River, Little Deschutes River, and Upper Klamath) are experiencing high to very high impacts due to ongoing hydrological changes based on the unified threats classification system ranking, described above. The altered hydrology has affected both breeding and wintering habitat, as discussed below.

Water Diversions/Manipulations— Dams in the upper watersheds of the Puget Trough, Willamette Valley, and the Deschutes River have significantly reduced the amount of shallow overflow wetland habitat that was historically created by natural flooding (Cushman and Pearl 2007, pp. 16-17). The inundation of large marsh complexes, and habitat fragmentation by the construction of reservoirs in the Cascades, has also eliminated and degraded Oregon spotted frog habitat. We are not aware of proposals for construction of new dams or reservoirs that would pose a threat to the existing Oregon spotted frog populations in British Columbia, Washington, or Oregon. However, the operation of existing dams/diversions/water control structures in Washington and Oregon continues to affect populations of Oregon spotted frogs due to extreme water fluctuations between and within years. These operations inundate and desiccate Oregon spotted frog habitat, while creating and maintaining habitat suitable for nonnative predaceous species.

Water management in the Glenwood Valley, Washington (Middle Klickitat River sub-basin), appears to be playing a significant role in the decline of the Oregon spotted frog in this sub-basin. Water management in this area is complex due to the juxtaposition of private, county, and federal lands, and the location and ownership of water diversion structures. The need to retain water on the Conboy Lake NWR for resources, including the Oregon spotted frog, conflicts with needs of the intermingled and adjacent private landowners who want water drawn down in order to grow reed canarygrass for haying or to graze cattle. In addition, water management on the NWR is constrained by failing dikes, plugged ditches, undersized culverts, and lack of water control structures (USFWS 2012, p. 27). Dewatering by Conboy Lake NWR generally begins June 1, but begins as early as April on privately held lands, which also results in the dewatering of some refuge lands (USFWS 2012, p. 28). The Camas Prairie area of the valley is drained annually to facilitate production of hay and grazing opportunities (USFWS 2012, p. 28).

Dewatering breeding areas during the egg stage results in desiccation of Oregon spotted frog egg masses. Dewatering during the rearing stage results in tadpole mortality if water is not retained through metamorphosis. Physical barriers created by the dike system hinder young frogs (recently metamorphosed) from moving into permanent waters, especially when water is drawn down too quickly or a surface water connection to permanent water is not retained. Disconnection from permanent water occurs in some places in the valley, which results in young frogs becoming stranded and dying. In the areas where a connection to permanent water is retained and frogs are able to move with the water, the frogs become concentrated in smaller areas with predators such as fish and bullfrogs or become easy targets for terrestrial predators (Engler 2006, pers. comm.). This issue is complex, because the nonnative bullfrog is fairly common on the refuge, and studies indicate they can prey heavily on native frog species, including Oregon spotted frog.

Water management can be used as a method to reduce bullfrog tadpole survival by drying up seasonal wetlands completely by early fall. However, widespread drawdowns for bullfrog tadpole control can conflict with the need to provide rearing, movement, and summertime water for Oregon spotted frogs (USFWS 2010b, pp. 36, 63, 67). Surveys since 1998 have documented extensive annual declines in Oregon spotted frog egg mass numbers due to early water drawdowns and perennially low water; therefore, inadequate water or poorly timed water management activities continue to be a threat to Oregon spotted frog that has a significant negative impact on recruitment (the addition of young individuals to the adult population) and survival in the Middle Klickitat River sub-basin.

In the Upper Deschutes River sub-basin in Oregon, regulated water releases from Crane Prairie and Wickiup Reservoirs result in extreme seasonal fluctuations in stream flows that have affected the amount of overwintering and breeding habitat available for Oregon spotted frogs. Prior to the construction of Wickiup Dam in 1947, the Deschutes River below the current dam site exhibited stable flows averaging approximately 730 cubic feet per second (cfs) (20.7 cubic meters per second (cms)) and 660 cfs (18.7 cms) during summer and winter, respectively (Hardin-Davis 1991). Water storage in the reservoirs during winter, water releases in the spring, and water diversions for irrigation result in extremely low winter flows (October through March) in the Deschutes River below Wickiup Dam of approximately 20-30 cfs (0.6-0.8 cms) and high summer flows (July and August) of approximately 1,400 cfs (39.6 cms). Because water releases from Wickiup Reservoir typically occur in early to mid-April, potential breeding habitats downstream of Wickiup Dam on the mainstem Deschutes River may not have sufficient water during the breeding season to facilitate frog movement and breeding unless supported by springs.

Currently, Oregon spotted frog breeding is known to occur in five areas downstream of Wickiup Reservoir along the Deschutes River: Dead Slough, La Pine State Park, Sunriver, Slough Camp, and Old Mill casting pond (including adjacent LSA marsh). Oregon spotted frog habitat at Sunriver Resort has been managed and maintained by Sunriver Nature Center by using weirs to stabilize the water levels from the beginning of the breeding season through metamorphosis, which has resulted in a large and fairly stable population of Oregon spotted frogs, despite the low river flows during the breeding season. Breeding and dispersal of metamorphosing frogs at the Slough Camp site is likely affected by the seasonal timing of storage and release of water from the reservoir each year. Adults have been observed at the inlet to Slough Camp (east side) prior to the flow releases from the reservoir in early April (Higgins 2012, pers. comm.), indicating that frogs may be staging to access breeding habitat that becomes accessible when flows are released for the irrigation season. At the onset of the storage season in October, the east side of Slough Camp drains rapidly of water, which could result in stranding of frogs that have bred and reared in this location. In 2012, Oregon spotted frogs were discovered in a water retention pond at The Old Mill District shops and in a riverine marsh (LSA marsh) across from the pond in downtown Bend, Oregon. The shallow pond, located within 20 ft (6 m) of the Deschutes River, is managed to provide year-round water that supports overwintering frogs. However, the impacts of regulated river flows to Oregon spotted frogs within the LSA marsh remain to be evaluated.

Oregon spotted frog habitat in the Little Deschutes River sub-basin in Oregon are affected by regulated water management downstream of Crescent Lake Dam in Crescent Creek and the Little Deschutes River below the confluence with Crescent Creek. Regulated water releases from Crescent Lake typically occur in June, just after the breeding season. Egg mass stranding has been observed on three separate occasions along the Little Deschutes River, downstream of the confluence with Crescent Creek, prior to the release of irrigation water (Demmer 2012, pers. comm.). Overwintering habitats may be limited when flows from Crescent Lake typically cease in October at the onset of the storage season. Groundwater may be ameliorating the impacts from the regulated water management in Crescent Creek in locations where groundwater discharges to the stream (Gannett et al. 2001), but a full analysis has not yet been conducted.

In the Klamath Basin, the Upper Klamath sub-basin populations may be affected by water diversion at Hyatt and Keene Creek dams. Hyatt and Keene Creek dams may divert up to 136 cfs of flow from Keene Creek, in the Klamath Basin, for agricultural, municipal and industrial, and hydroelectric power generation in the Rogue basin (OWRD 2002, 2008). While there is no known surface or subsurface connection between the operation of these facilities and Oregon spotted frog populations in the Parsnip Lakes, these dams may affect flows in Keene Creek, where isolated juvenile Oregon spotted frogs have been observed (Parker 2009, p. 5). The precise effect of water diversion at these facilities on habitat conditions is unknown and has been complicated by grazing practices and the loss of beaver dams in the area (Parker 2009, p. 5). While these facilities reduce Keene Creek flows during the winter and spring, groundwater contributions from Keene Creek reservoir may contribute to wetland conditions during dry summer conditions.

Development—Other hydrological changes result from the development of homes and roads adjacent to wetlands with Oregon spotted frogs. Development introduces new impervious surfaces, which increase the amplitude and frequencies of peak highs and lows in water levels, a hydrologic characteristic that has been implicated in reduced amphibian species diversity in wetlands in King County, Washington (Richter and Azous 1995, p. 308). (See "Development" section below for further discussion.) Manmade barriers (e.g., culverts) on roads that intersect streams, rivers, and/or wetlands that disconnect or increase the amplitude of flow may prevent or impede Oregon spotted frog movements between breeding areas and other habitats. However, the extent or severity of this threat is not determinable at this time.

Drought—Changes in water levels due to drought, and exacerbated by human modification, have caused seasonal loss of habitat and degradation of essential shoreline vegetation that has resulted in reduced recruitment regionally (Licht 1971, p. 122; Licht 1974, p. 623). In 1997, Hayes identified 14 of 24 (58 percent) Oregon spotted frog breeding locations across the extant range as having a moderate to high risk from drought (1997, pp. 43-45). Drought risk was based on the potential for a drop in water level that could reduce or eliminate the species' habitat. Sites with the greatest risk included those sites with low precipitation levels and sites dependent upon surface flow rather than flow from springs. Sites with the greatest risk from drought are in the Klamath and Deschutes River basins of Oregon (Hayes 1997, p. 44; Hayes et al. 1997, p. 6). The impact of a drought on an Oregon spotted frog population depends on the amount of complex marsh habitat at a site, the availability of alternative breeding and rearing areas, and the abundance of aquatic predators (Pearl 1999, p. 15).

Low water levels resulting from drought may reduce populations of nonnative predators (fish and bullfrogs); however, both Hayes (1997, p. 43) and Pearl (1999, pp. 17-18) hypothesized that low water conditions will increase the overlap between Oregon spotted frogs and nonnative predators, such as brook trout and bullfrogs, by concentrating tadpoles and froglets in the only available habitat. Such increased overlap is expected to increase predation losses of Oregon spotted frogs (Pearl et al. 2004, pp. 17-18). Several seasons of low water are expected to cause local population extirpations of Oregon spotted frogs, particularly where a small isolated population occupies a limited marsh habitat that has a high abundance of aquatic predators (Pearl 1999, p. 15). Low water in breeding habitat will also expose eggs to increased ultraviolet radiation and higher mortality associated with pathogens (Kiesecker et al. 2001a, p. 682) (see "Disease" under Factor C section). Since 1960, the Klamath Basin has had 8 of the 10 lowest inflows for Upper Klamath Lake between 1991 and 2009 (USFWS 2011a, p. 25). This has resulted in poor water quality and reduced Oregon spotted frog reproduction due to desiccation of egg masses (BLM and USFS multiple data sources). In addition, 5 of the 10 sites in the Klamath Basin are vulnerable to water management practices that are timed such that the seasonal life-history needs of the Oregon spotted frog are not met.

Although the Chemult Ranger District, Fremont-Winema National Forest, in Klamath County, Oregon, documented high numbers of egg masses at Jack Creek in 1999 and 2000 (335 and 320 respectively) (Forbes and Peterson 1999, p. 6), drought conditions impacted the Oregon spotted frog populations in subsequent years. The drought occurred during the time period in which the Oregon spotted frog population dramatically declined at Jack Creek (Gervais 2011, p. 15). In 2001, those conditions restricted Oregon spotted frog breeding to three small, disjunct areas representing less than 25 percent of their typical habitat. Although there were sufficient water depths in the breeding pools in 2002, only 17 percent of historical egg mass numbers were detected, and 50 percent of the eggs did not hatch compared to the 68 to 74 percent hatch rates documented by Licht (1974, p. 618). The impacts of the drought were further complicated when Oregon spotted frog habitat was impacted by algal blooms, poor water quality, loss of protective habitat, and alteration of the bank condition (USDA 2009a, pp. 31, 33-34). By 2011, only 1 percent of historical egg mass numbers were documented at this site.

Loss of Beaver—The American beaver (Castor canadensis) creates a complex mosaic of aquatic habitat types that provides the seasonal habitat needs of the Oregon spotted frog. Water impoundments created and engineered by beavers result in a water storage reservoir that raises the water table, reduces downstream erosion, lessens flood events (unless the dam is breached), holds water year round, and maintains stream flow during dry periods. Specifically, silt-filled abandoned ponds become shallow wetlands and beaver meadows, which have characteristics ideal for egg-laying. Beaver-maintained ponds retain deeper waters important for summer foraging and growth of metamorphosed frogs, and these ponds also provide overwintering habitat. When hypoxic conditions occur in the wetlands and ponds, the frogs can move to the more oxygenated waters of the associated creek, where they use microhabitat features created by beavers such as large woody debris and bank tunnels (Hallock and Pearson 2001, pp. 9-12; Shovlain 2005, p. 10).

Comparisons of beaver-occupied and not occupied watersheds in Montana in relation to Columbia spotted frog populations found: (a) Beaver watersheds had four times as many lentic and breeding sites as non-beaver watersheds; (b) frog breeding sites were dispersed within beaver drainages, while non-beaver watersheds often had only one frog breeding site; (c) frog breeding sites were evenly distributed across the elevational gradient in beaver watersheds, while they were centered above the watershed midpoint in non-beaver watersheds; (d) frog breeding sites were more dispersed within drainages with evidence of beaver presence than would be expected given the configuration of the underlying lentic habitat and have persisted despite being separated by distances larger than the frog's dispersal ability; (e) beaver watersheds with an average distance of less than 3.1 mi (5 km) between breeding sites showed higher levels of connectivity than did non-beaver watersheds with an average distance of more than 3.1 mi (5 km) between breeding sites; and (f) short beaver watersheds had lower levels of genetic divergence between breeding sites than those in long non-beaver watersheds separated by the same distance, even when distances were within the commonly observed dispersal ability of the frogs (Amish 2006, entire). Columbia and Oregon spotted frogs were separated into two separate species (Rana pretiosa (Oregon spotted frog) and Rana luteiventris (Columbia spotted frog)), based on genetic analysis (Green et al. 1996, 1997). They are closely related species and likely evolved in a similar way, with beavers playing a vital role in how frogs are distributed within a watershed.

By 1900, beavers had been nearly extirpated in the continental United States (Baker and Hill 2003, p. 288). Beavers have made a remarkable comeback in many areas through natural recolonization and relocation efforts (ODFW 2012, p. 1); however, their role as ecological engineers is still severely curtailed region-wide, particularly within human-populated areas, because they are often considered a pest species because they can flood roads and property and destroy trees that are valued by landowners (Baker and Hill 2003, p. 301). In at least one site, a significant Oregon spotted frog decline was attributed to the removal of a series of beaver dams that resulted in water loss within some of the breeding areas leading to high embryo mortality attributed to stranding (Hayes et al. 2000, p. 2). In Trout Lake Creek in Washington, the loss of a beaver dam to a natural flood event resulted in a significant decline (117 egg masses in 2001 to 0 in 2012) in Oregon spotted frog reproduction (Hallock 2012, p. 33). Lack of beavers within a watershed has been determined by USFS and BLM to be a threat to maintenance of Oregon spotted frog habitat, and these agencies have identified the Williamson, Upper Klamath Lake, and Upper Klamath sub-basins for reintroduction of beaver to aid Oregon spotted frogs.

The States of Washington and Oregon allow lethal removal of beavers and their dams. Under Washington State law, the beaver is classified as a furbearer (WAC 232-12-007). The owner, the owner's immediate family, an employee, or a tenant of property may shoot or trap a beaver on that property if a threat to crops exists (RCW 77.36.030). In such cases, no special trapping permit is necessary for the use of live traps. However, a special trapping permit is required for the use of all traps other than live traps (RCW 77.15.192, 77.15.194; WAC 232-12-142). It is unlawful to release a beaver anywhere within Washington, other than on the property where it was legally trapped, without a permit to do so (RCW 77.15.250; WAC 232-12-271). To remove or modify a beaver dam, one must have a Hydraulic Project Approval—a permit issued by Washington Department of Fish and Wildlife (WDFW) for work that will use, obstruct, change, or divert the bed or flow of State waters (RCW 77.55). Beavers are present to a varying degree within all Oregon spotted frog occupied sub-basins in Washington and are maintaining breeding habitats in some areas within the South Fork Nooksack River, Black River, White Salmon River, and Middle Klickitat River sub-basins. Active removal of beavers or their dams is occurring in at least the South Fork Nooksack River, Black River, and Middle Klickitat River sub-basins and may be occurring in the other occupied sub-basins in Washington.

Beavers on public lands in Oregon are classified as Protected Furbearers by Oregon Revised Statute (ORS) 496.004 and Oregon Administrative Rule (OAR) 635-050-0050. A trapping license and open season are required to trap beavers on public lands. Beavers on private lands are defined as a Predatory Animal (ORS 610.002) and private landowners or their agents may lethally remove beavers without a permit from the Oregon Department of Fish and Wildlife (ODFW). Currently, the presence of beavers results in active maintenance of Oregon spotted frog habitat in the Little Deschutes River, Upper Deschutes River, Middle Fork Willamette River, Williamson River, and Upper Klamath Lake sub-basins. Active removal of beavers and their dams can occur in the Oregon spotted frog habitat in all of these occupied sub-basins in Oregon. Under State laws in both Washington and Oregon, it is lawful to kill beavers or to remove or modify beaver dams, and those lawful actions reduce or degrade wetland habitats used by all life stages of Oregon spotted frogs.

Hydrologic Changes Conclusion— A variety of factors affecting the hydrology of wetlands and riverine systems cause the loss or detrimental modification of habitats necessary for the survival and reproduction of Oregon spotted frogs. Within 11 of the 15 sub-basins occupied by the species, water diversions/manipulations, development, drought, and loss of beavers are resulting in hydrological changes that pose a threat to all life stages of the Oregon spotted frog, including loss of or disconnections between breeding, rearing, and overwintering habitat, as well as desiccation or flooding of egg masses. The impact to Oregon spotted frogs of these hydrological changes has been determined—based on our unified threats classification system (Threats Synthesis Rangewide Analysis)—to be moderate to very high in five of the occupied sub-basins: Middle Klickitat River, Upper Deschutes River, Little Deschutes River, Williamson River, and Upper Klamath.

Changes in Vegetation

Oregon spotted frog egg-laying sites are generally characterized by low vegetation canopy coverage and a substrate at least partially covered with the previous year's emergent herbaceous vegetation (Leonard 1997, p. 3; Hayes et al. 2000, p. 8; Pearl and Bury 2000, p. 6; Pearl 1999, p. 15). Egg masses are generally found in shallow water over vegetation and are rarely found above open soil or rocky substrates (Hayes et al. 2000, p. 8, Pearl and Bury 2000, p. 8). Watson et al. (2003, p. 296) found that habitat selection by Oregon spotted frogs during the breeding season was strongly correlated with sedge habitat in Washington. In Oregon, Pearl et al. (2009a, p.141) found the dominant vegetation at egg-laying areas to be sedge-rush habitat.

Loss of natural wetland and riverine disturbance processes as a result of human activities has caused, and continues to cause, degradation of Oregon spotted frog habitat. Historically, a number of natural forces created emergent wetlands favorable to Oregon spotted frogs. These forces included rivers meandering over their floodplains, removing trees and shrubs and baring patches of mineral soil; beavers felling trees and woody shrubs, trampling vegetation, and dragging limbs and logs through shallows; and summer fires burning areas that would be shallow water wetlands during the Oregon spotted frog breeding season the following spring. Today, all of these forces are greatly reduced, impaired, or have been permanently altered as a result of human activities. In addition, the current wetland management paradigm is generally a no-management approach that often results in continued invasion by invasive plants or succession to a tree- and shrub-dominated community, both of which are unsuitable for Oregon spotted frog breeding.

Invasive plants such as reed canarygrass may completely change the structure of wetland environments, and can create dense areas of vegetation unsuitable as Oregon spotted frog habitat (McAllister and Leonard 1997, p. 23). Reed canarygrass competitively excludes other native plant species and limits the biological and habitat diversity of host wetland and riparian habitats (Antieau 1998, p. 2). Reed canarygrass also removes large quantities of water through evapotranspiration, potentially affecting shallow groundwater hydrologic characteristics (Antieau 1998, p. 2). Reed canarygrass dominates large areas of Oregon spotted frog habitat at lower elevations (Hayes 1997, p. 44; Hayes et al. 1997, p. 6) and is broadening its range to high-elevation (i.e., above 4,500 feet (>1,371 m)) Oregon spotted frog habitat in the Little Deschutes and Upper Deschutes River sub-basins in Oregon (USDA 2008, USDA 2009b, USDA 2009c, and USDA 2011b). Watson et al. (2003, p. 296) compared the types and amount of habitat used by Oregon spotted frogs and found the frogs used areas of reed canarygrass less frequently than other habitats based on availability. Given this apparent avoidance of reed canarygrass, vegetation shifts to reed canarygrass dominance in wetlands occupied by Oregon spotted frogs are likely affecting Oregon spotted frog breeding behavior.

Studies conducted in Washington (White 2002, pp. 45-46; Pearl and Hayes 2004, pp. 22-23) demonstrated that the quality of breeding habitats for Oregon spotted frogs is improved by reducing the height of the previous years' emergent vegetation (i.e., reed canarygrass in these cases). However, improvement in breeding habitat for Oregon spotted frogs was retained only if vegetation management was maintained. For example, in all occupied sub-basins in Washington and in the Klamath sub-basin in Oregon, an indirect effect of the removal of cattle grazing has been the reduction in the amount and quality of breeding and rearing habitat due to encroachment by vegetation, such as reed canarygrass and shrubs. The effects of grazing vary among sites and likely depend on a suite of factors including, but not limited to, timing, intensity, duration, and how these factors interact with seasonal habitat use patterns of Oregon spotted frog.

Reed canarygrass is present at three of the British Columbia breeding areas and is the dominant vegetation at most of the breeding areas in Washington. In Oregon, reed canarygrass is colonizing portions of Big Marsh and Little Lava Lake, both of which are headwaters to the Little Deschutes and Upper Deschutes River sub-basins, respectively. Reed canarygrass also is present in Oregon spotted frog habitat at Lava Lake, Davis Lake, Wickiup Reservoir, multiple sites along the Little Deschutes River (i.e., 7 out of 13 surveyed sites), Slough Camp, Wood River Wetland, the Klamath Marsh NWR, Fourmile Creek, and the Williamson River. The impact to Oregon spotted frogs due to habitat loss from reed canarygrass invasion has been determined through our threat analyses to be high to very high in seven sub-basins: Lower Fraser River in British Columbia and all sub-basins in Washington. The effects of reed canarygrass to Oregon spotted frog habitat are considered to be moderate in two sub-basins in Oregon: Little Deschutes River and Upper Deschutes River.

Vegetation succession was indicated as a negative factor at almost all remaining Oregon spotted frog sites analyzed by Hayes, who noted that some sites were particularly vulnerable to habitat loss where marsh-to-meadow changes were occurring (Hayes 1997, p. 45). Pearl (1999, p. 15) suggested that the aquatic habitat types necessary for Oregon spotted frog reproductive sites in lake basins exist only within a narrow successional window. As marsh size decreases due to plant succession, shallow warm water sites required by Oregon spotted frogs are lost to increased shading by woody vegetation (Pearl 1999, pp. 15-16). Investigations by Hayes (1997, p. 45) and Pearl (1999, p. 16) ranked 22 of 28 Oregon spotted frog sites as having a moderate or high threat from vegetation succession. Encroachment around and into marshes by lodgepole pine and other woody vegetation is occurring at Conboy Lake in Washington (Ludwig 2011, p. 3) and at multiple breeding locations in Oregon, and is likely facilitated by ditching and draining of wetter sites to improve grazing (Cushman and Pearl 2007, p. 17). The highest impact to Oregon spotted frogs resulting from lodgepole pine encroachment is taking place in the Upper Deschutes River sub-basin and in the upper elevations of the Little Deschutes River sub-basin in Oregon, where these breeding habitats (i.e., those within the riparian lodgepole plant association group), evolved with fire as a natural disturbance process. The loss of natural fire cycles in forests of the eastern Cascade Mountains due to suppression on National Forest land since 1910 (Agee 1993, p. 58) has allowed succession to continue without disturbance. Plot data suggest that historical fire return intervals for riparian lodgepole pine vegetation types in central Oregon ranged from 12 to 36 years and averaged 24 years (Simpson 2007, p. 9-6), indicating that this disturbance process was more frequent historically in this forest type.

The United States Department of Agriculture's Natural Resources Conservation Service (NRCS) and Farm Service Agency have several voluntary programs, including the Wetland Reserve Program (WRP), CREP, and Wildlife Habitat Incentive Program. The WRP and CREP are voluntary programs designed to help landowners address concerns regarding the use of natural resources and promote landowner conservation. Under the WRP, landowners enter into a voluntary agreement with NRCS to protect, restore, and enhance wetlands on their property. Various enrollment options are available to landowners, including Permanent Easements, 30-Year Easements, Restoration Cost-Share Agreements, or 30-Year Contracts (USDA NRCS 2013). Under the CREP, the Farm Service Agency provides payments to landowners who sign a contract committing to keeping lands out of agricultural production for a period of 10 to 15 years. NRCS produces technical guidelines generally aimed at improving soil conditions, agricultural productivity, and water quality, which generally do not result in specific conservation measures for the protection of the Oregon spotted frog. Rather, restoration actions funded or carried out by NRCS include planting trees and shrubs in riparian areas.

These activities have had unforeseen consequences to Oregon spotted frog habitat by degrading breeding habitat because, as discussed above, tree- and shrub-dominated communities are unsuitable for Oregon spotted frog breeding. This is known to have occurred within the last 10 years at breeding locations in Black, Samish, and South Fork Nooksack Rivers in Washington (Nisqually NWR; Bohannon et al. 2012) and may be happening elsewhere. Currently, one known occupied private land parcel has entered into a WRP agreement in the Klamath Basin in Oregon. The WRP agreement for this particular parcel allows no grazing in perpetuity, which, in the long term, may result in reduced quality of Oregon spotted frog habitat. We are aware of at least one CREP contract in the South Fork Nooksack River sub-basin that resulted in conifer tree plantings in Oregon spotted frog breeding locations, which resulted in the wetted areas becoming drier and mostly shaded. The Service has had preliminary discussions with NRCS and is working with the agency to address this management issue.

Changes in vegetation conclusion— Expansion of reed canarygrass into Oregon spotted frog habitat poses a threat to the continued existence of these habitats given the invasive nature of the plant and its ability to outcompete native vegetation in wetland habitats. Shallow water wetlands inhabited by Oregon spotted frog are threatened through rapid encroachment of the grass and increased evapotranspiration of water. Loss of habitat at breeding sites due to reed canarygrass is high to very high in seven occupied sub-basins in British Columbia and Washington. Reed canarygrass poses a threat in the Little Deschutes and Upper Deschutes River sub-basins in Oregon, and is present at varying abundances in many locations occupied by Oregon spotted frog.

Vegetation succession, particularly where natural disturbance processes are lacking, is a negative factor at almost all Oregon spotted frog sites. Structural changes to vegetation that occur through succession, whether from native or nonnative grasses, shrubs, or trees, results in decreased wetland size and amount of open water area available to frogs. Furthermore, shrub and tree encroachment increases shading of shallow warm water sites required by Oregon spotted frogs for breeding and rearing. Encroachment by lodgepole pine and other woody vegetation is occurring at multiple breeding locations in Washington and Oregon and is considered a threat in at least seven sub-basins: Lower Deschutes River, Upper Deschutes River, McKenzie River, Middle Fork Willamette River, Williamson River, Upper Klamath Lake, and Upper Klamath. Unintended loss of habitat is taking place as a result of riparian restoration activities that remove grazing and plant shrubs and trees within sub-basins occupied by Oregon spotted frogs in Washington and Oregon. Therefore, based on the best scientific information available, changes in vegetation pose a threat to Oregon spotted frogs due to habitat loss and modification throughout the range of the species.

Development

Removal or alteration of natural riparian vegetation around watercourses or wetlands for urban or agricultural development compromises aquatic ecosystem function via reductions in biodiversity and water quality and quantity. Residential and commercial encroachment often destroys or disturbs natural vegetation, alters water flows and seasonal flooding, or results in the loss of entire wetland complexes. Agricultural practices, including grazing, can result in the rapid removal of water across the landscape for stimulation of early grass production. All of these factors have been shown to reduce the survival and reproductive capacity of Oregon spotted frogs, as discussed previously.

Although the historical impact of development has significantly reduced the abundance and geographic distributions of Oregon spotted frogs (for example, the Fraser River Valley in British Columbia, Puget Trough in Washington, and Willamette Valley in Oregon), development is currently an ongoing threat at only a few specific locations. In British Columbia, housing and residential developments continue to remove or alter habitat at Mountain and Maria Sloughs, and there are new commercial developments at Mountain Slough (COSFRT 2012, p. 26).

In Washington, some counties prohibit draining of wetlands and some counties require setbacks from wetlands (see Factor D for further information), but this is not consistent, nor consistently implemented. In addition, a large proportion of the breeding areas for Oregon spotted frogs in Washington is not technically classified as a wetland under the county definitions because these areas are seasonally flooded pastures. The private lands surrounding breeding areas for the Oregon spotted frog in most of the occupied sub-basins are presently zoned as rural or rural residential, which is designed only to allow low-density housing and maintain the rural and agricultural uses. However, the human populations of all counties in the Puget Sound area are growing and Thurston, Whatcom, and Skagit Counties have the 6th, 9th, and 10th largest populations, respectively, among Washington State's 39 counties (U.S. Census Bureau data downloaded August 29, 2012). Between 1990 and 2011, the populations in these three counties have doubled. This population increase is expected to continue, resulting in new residential and commercial developments that are likely to alter vegetation, water flow, and the seasonal flooding that creates and maintains habitat for Oregon spotted frogs.

Development of land along the Little Deschutes River and its tributaries in Oregon is a continued threat to the Oregon spotted frog due to loss or modification of its habitat. The rural character of the Little Deschutes River watershed, the attractive location of private property on the Little Deschutes River, and relatively inexpensive land prices have contributed to a rapidly growing population (UDWC 2002, p. 12). In the 1960s and 1970s before Oregon Statewide planning regulated growth and development, 15,000 one- and two-acre lots were created in subdivisions in the vicinity of the Little Deschutes River. Since 1989, Deschutes County has been the fastest growing county in Oregon on a percentage basis. The unincorporated areas of Deschutes County, including the lower portions of the Little Deschutes River, are projected to increase in population size by as much as 56 percent above the 2000 level over the next 20 years (UDWC 2002, p. 12). This rapid population growth rate is expected to continue into the future (UDWC 2002, p. 12), thereby increasing risks to wetland habitats that support Oregon spotted frogs in the vicinity of the Little Deschutes River.

Development in the Klamath Basin is also increasing in Oregon. The population of Klamath County increased 10.5 percent from 1990 to 2000 (U.S. Census Bureau 2008) and annual housing starts have increased by 13 percent since 2000 (Portland State University 2011 Web site). Much of the growth is outside of city boundaries, and several large residential developments are within or adjacent to wetlands that historically had the ability to support Oregon spotted frog habitat. In addition, agricultural practices, including grazing, occur extensively within all three occupied sub-basins. This has the potential to result in the desiccation or inundation of Oregon spotted frog habitat (see the "Oregon" discussion under "Livestock Grazing," below). While it is unknown to what extent urban development has impacted Oregon spotted frog habitat, agricultural development is ongoing and continues to impact Oregon spotted frog habitat.

Development conclusion— Development of residential, commercial, and agricultural properties is continuing in at least 10 of the sub-basins occupied by the Oregon spotted frog. In some areas, the human population is expected to continue to grow. Development activities directly and indirectly have removed or altered habitat necessary to support all life stages of Oregon spotted frogs. Therefore, we consider development—both at the present time and in the future—to be a threat to the Oregon spotted frog due to loss or modification of its habitat.

Livestock Grazing

In several riparian zones and wetland complexes in British Columbia, Washington, and Oregon, livestock grazing occurs within Oregon spotted frog habitat, although its effects vary with the site conditions, livestock numbers, timing, and intensity. Livestock (primarily horses and cows) can cause direct mortality by trampling adult frogs (Ross et al. 1999, p. 163) and egg masses when livestock are allowed in shallow water habitat when frogs are present. Livestock graze and trample emergent and riparian vegetation, compact soil in riparian and upland areas, and reduce bank stability, which results in increased sedimentation and water pollution via urine and feces (Hayes 1997, p. 44; Hayes 1998b, p. 8; 61 FR 25813). The resulting increases in temperature and sediment production, alterations to stream morphology, effects on prey organisms, and changes in water quality negatively affect Oregon spotted frog habitat. Livestock trampling compacts affected soils and decreases soil porosity, which results in reduced water holding capacity (Kauffman and Krueger 1984, p. 434). Livestock also act as vectors for the introduction of weed seeds that alter riparian vegetation characteristics (Belsky and Gelbard 2000, p. 9), and they are a source of introduced parasites and pathogens (see Factor C discussion).

Fourteen of twenty-eight (50 percent) sites surveyed in British Columbia, Washington, and

Oregon were directly or indirectly influenced (negatively and positively) by livestock grazing (Hayes 1997, p. 44; Hayes et al. 1997, p. 6; Pearl 1999, p. 16). Severe habitat modification has been caused by cattle at several Oregon spotted frog localities in Oregon. Large numbers of cattle at a site negatively affect habitat for Oregon spotted frogs, particularly at springs used by frogs as overwintering sites (Hayes 1997, p. 44). However, in recent work monitoring the effects of livestock grazing on Oregon spotted frogs in grazed and ungrazed treatments at Jack Creek on the Fremont Winema National Forests in Oregon, Shovlain (2009, entire) suggested that Oregon spotted frogs did not modify their habitat use in response to increased grazing pressure in summer-time habitats. However, Shovlain's analyses may have been affected by a relatively low sample size and unbalanced data, the inability to account for frog habitat use outside of the plots, as well as the possibility that the frog's habitat use was related to the availability of water rather than vegetation density or livestock effects (Shovlain 2009, pp. 11-12). In summer-time habitat, livestock, in particular cattle, may increase Oregon spotted frog's susceptibility to desiccation and trampling if both frogs and livestock are using the same remnant pools. In addition, cattle can impact the quantity of available water. A cow can drink 15 to 20 gallons of water per day (Engle 2002, cited in USDA 2004, p. 31). For example, Jack Creek and its tributaries provide the only sustained water to cow-calf pairs within the Jack Creek grazing allotment, and the cows are on the allotment for about 100 days per year (USDA 2004, p. 31). During drought years, such as 2000 through 2004 (see "Drought" discussion, above), the remnant pools, with the added pressure of livestock, may dry up, resulting in frogs being stranded and desiccating.

Moderate livestock grazing can, in some instances (for example, Dempsey Creek in Washington), benefit Oregon spotted frogs by maintaining openings in the vegetation in highly altered wetland communities (Hayes 1997, p. 44; Hayes et al. 1997, p. 6; McAllister and Leonard 1997, p. 25). Watson et al. (2003, p. 299) found that habitat at 78 percent of the Oregon spotted frog locations surveyed at the Dempsey Creek site had signs of grazing, which created penetrable, open habitat that was otherwise too dense for frog use.

British Columbia— Only one known breeding location (Morris Valley) in the Lower Fraser River sub-basin is grazed (by horses) (COSEWIC 2011, p. 33), and grazing is identified as a specific concern for Oregon spotted frogs at this location because of the potential for trampling of egg masses, bank erosion, and input of feces (COSEWIC 2011, p. 33).

Washington— In the recent past, it appears that grazing was beneficial to Oregon spotted frogs at all remaining breeding areas in Washington; however, grazing no longer occurs in the breeding areas in four of the six sub-basins due to land manager preferences and/or water quality regulations that prohibit grazing within certain distances from rivers and wetlands. Active management is required to maintain the Oregon spotted frog habitat at these locations due to heavy reed canarygrass infestations, but funding is limited and grazing had been the least expensive and easiest management option. In the Black River, grazing ceased along Dempsey Creek when the privately owned dairy operation was sold. Cows were reintroduced to the Port Blakely Tree Farm and Musgrove (Nisqually NWR) parcels in 2008 (USFWS 2011b), as part of a reed canarygrass control experiment; however, Oregon spotted frog egg mass numbers have not increased as was expected (WDFW 2011 database; USFWS 2011b). Grazing occurs at the only known breeding location in the Lower Chilliwack River sub-basin. This site has likely persisted as a result of dairy cows maintaining the site in a state of early seral habitat (Bohannon et al. 2012, p. 17).

Oregon—Overgrazing of the Camas Prairie in Oregon was considered a threat to Oregon spotted frog prior to 2008, after which grazing was restricted (Corkran 2012). Overgrazing by cattle reduced the vegetative hiding cover for frogs, making them more susceptible to predation. Livestock-induced fertilization resulted in an increased density of the aquatic vegetation, which inhibited the ability of frogs to drop below the water's surface when threatened by predation while basking (Corkran 2012, pers. comm). However, grazing may be considered as a management tool to maintain early seral habitat for Oregon spotted frogs in the future if necessary (Corkran 2012, pers. comm).

None of the central Oregon Cascade breeding locations within the Deschutes and Willamette National Forests is within grazing allotments. Known breeding locations occur within allotments on the BLM Prineville District lands along Crescent Creek, Long Prairie Creek, and the Little Deschutes River. Currently, only the Crescent Creek area is affected by active grazing on BLM lands, although there is potential for grazing to occur on BLM lands along the Little Deschutes River. Grazing has been cited as an impact to riparian and wetland habitats on private lands along the Little Deschutes River (The Wetlands Conservancy, 2004, p. 22). Wetland habitats in the Little Deschutes River sub-basin have been negatively impacted by grazing through removal of riparian vegetation, which destabilizes banks and increases channel incision, resulting in less water retention in riparian wetlands and conifer encroachment (UDWC 2002, pp. 21 and 53).

Six sites in the Klamath Basin are associated with grazing: Jack Creek, Buck Lake, Parsnip Lakes, and on private lands on the Wood River, Williamson River, and adjacent to Klamath Marsh NWR. These sites are potentially vulnerable to both the direct impacts of grazing sedimentation, trampling, as well as the indirect effect of egg mass desiccation resulting from water management techniques that drain water early in frog breeding season to stimulate grass production. Livestock grazing is cited as a specific concern for Oregon spotted frogs at Jack Creek, Fremont-Winema National Forest, Chemult Ranger District, in Oregon (USDA 2004, pp. 56-57). Since 1999, the population has reduced from 670 breeding adults (335 egg masses) to 34 breeding adults (17 egg masses) in 2011. The two primary breeding sites in Jack Creek occur on private land that is heavily grazed in combination with USFS allotments. This intensity of grazing is expected to have degraded the quality of the Oregon spotted frog breeding habitat and reduced reproduction (Shovlain 2005).

Since 2008, current USFS management at the Jack Creek site has not permitted cattle grazing on lands occupied by Oregon spotted frogs (Markus 2012, pers. comm.). However, 419 cow/calf pairs specifically permitted for grazing have access to 61 ac (25 ha) of potential, but not currently supporting, Oregon spotted frog habitat on this 68,349-ac (27,660-ha) combination of USFS and private pasture. Within this pasture, however, there are several riparian areas accessible to grazing cattle as well as one offsite watering source installed on adjacent private land. The permittee for this pasture has grazed their private lands where Oregon spotted frogs are known to occur, although the number of cattle and timing are not known. However, the permittee has also partnered with the Service to complete multiple conservation actions to benefit Oregon spotted frogs and their habitats on their private lands including—but not limited to—the installation of 2 to 3 offsite watering sources, protection of frog ponds, thinning of encroaching lodgepole pine trees, and installation of a wattle for water retention (Markus 2012, pers. comm.).

Conflicts between cattle and frogs increase when stream flows are limited, especially when cattle are using the creek for drinking (Gervais 2011, p. 15). Between 2001 and 2005, and again in 2007, drought conditions affected habitat for Oregon spotted frogs in the Chemult Ranger District, Fremont-Winema National Forest in Oregon. However, until 2008, when grazing was restricted, 419 cow/calf pairs had access to the habitat areas associated with Oregon spotted frogs (Gervais 2011, p. 11). Cattle were observed congregating in Oregon spotted frog habitat because nearly every other water source in the allotment went dry (Simpson 2002, pers. comm.). Trampling of frogs by cattle and alterations in water quality, bank structure, and loss of protective vegetation compounded the impacts of the reduction of available habitat due to drought conditions on Oregon spotted frog reproduction (USDA 2009a, pp. 31, 33-34).

Livestock Grazing Conclusion— Where livestock grazing coincides with Oregon spotted frog habitat, impacts to the species include trampling of frogs and changes in habitat quality due to increased sedimentation, increased water temperatures, water management techniques, and reduced water quality. The effects of livestock grazing vary with site conditions, livestock numbers, and timing and intensity of grazing. In Washington, all of the known occupied areas have been grazed in the recent past, but where grazing has been removed, heavy infestations by invasive reed canarygrass have reduced or eliminated habitat for Oregon spotted frogs unless other management techniques were applied. In controlled circumstances, moderate grazing can be beneficial if it is the only practical method for controlling invasive, nonnative vegetation and sustaining short vegetation characteristics needed for egg laying. Grazing is ongoing in 10 of the occupied sub-basins and is considered to be a threat to Oregon spotted frogs at these locations.

Conservation Efforts To Reduce Habitat Destruction, Modification, or Curtailment of Its Range

British Columbia— Past and ongoing habitat conservation activities in British Columbia include habitat creation at MD Aldergrove, Maria Slough, and Mountain Slough; habitat rehabilitation at Maria and Mountain Sloughs; and invasive grass species management at MD Aldergrove, Maria Slough, and Mountain Slough. There also is a landowner stewardship contact program that encourages stewardship activities at Mountain Slough. However, the Service concluded that these measures are not sufficient to ameliorate threats to Oregon spotted frogs in the Lower Fraser River.

Washington— In Washington, some reed canarygrass management is taking place at most of the breeding locations in the Black River, on the Trout Lake NAP, and at Conboy Lake NWR. These management techniques include mowing, burning, cattle grazing, and shade cloth. However, these management techniques are not widespread at any one location or adequate to prevent loss of egg-laying habitat.

Conboy Lake NWR in Washington has completed several wetland restoration projects to restore natural hydrological processes to portions of the refuge. This enabled the NWR to maintain independent water management of several wetlands, regardless of the water-related impacts of local landowners. However, under current management, water is not retained throughout the year on most of the NWR and adjacent private wetlands, and many of these areas that had Oregon spotted frogs in the late 1990s no longer have Oregon spotted frogs.

Cattle grazing ceased at Trout Lake NAP in Washington after a monitoring study showed no apparent positive effect on the Oregon spotted frog population trends (Wilderman and Hallock 2004, p. 10), indicating either that grazing was not an effective tool for reed canarygrass management at this location, or that perhaps reed canarygrass was not as threatening to breeding frogs at this location as previously thought. This may be because winter snow pack flattens the reed canarygrass, creating a mostly sun-exposed water surface available to Oregon spotted frogs during the breeding season. The observed negative consequences of grazing, while perhaps acceptable if there was clear benefit to the Oregon spotted frog populations, were not compatible with other site management goals and posed a limitation to future restoration on the site (Wilderman and Hallock 2004, p. 14). Instead, problematic areas of reed canarygrass are being managed using ground barriers and occasional fall mowing (Hallock 2012, p. 31).

Under the Washington State Forest Practices Act, Washington Department of Natural Resources (WDNR) must approve certain activities related to growing, harvesting, or processing timber on all local government, State, and privately owned forest lands. WDNR's mission is to protect public resources while maintaining a viable timber industry. The primary goal of the forest practices rules is to achieve protection of water quality, fish and wildlife habitat, and capital improvements while ensuring that harvested areas are reforested. Presently, the Washington State Forest Practices Rules do not specifically protect Oregon spotted frogs; however, they do include protection measures for surface waters and wetlands. The intent of the protection measures, such as buffers on wetlands, is to limit excess coarse and fine sediment delivery and to maintain hydrologic regimes. Tree harvest is limited in wetland buffers, which may in turn facilitate vegetation encroachment. Landowners have the option to develop a management plan for the species if it resides on their property, or if landowners choose not to develop a management plan for the species with WDFW, their forest practices application will be conditioned to protect this public resource. While the Washington State Forest Practices Rules provide some protections for the Oregon spotted frog and its habitat, the direct and indirect consequences of limiting tree harvest within the wetland buffer is vegetation encroachment that is resulting in loss of wetlands (i.e., reduced size) and shading.

NRCS is overseeing the restoration at two Samish River locations and is incorporating Oregon spotted frog breeding habitat requirements into its planned restoration (that originally included de-leveling and tree and shrub plantings in the breeding areas) (Bohannan et al. 2012, p. 17).

Oregon—In Oregon, several conservation actions have been and continue to be implemented for Oregon spotted frogs in the Deschutes River Basin. Sunriver Nature Center has been monitoring the frog population at the Sunriver Resort since 2000. Although this area is affected by the fluctuating flows out of Wickiup Reservoir, Sunriver Nature Center has constructed weirs that allow the water level to be steady or rising from the time of egg-laying through hatching, thus assisting the persistence of this large and stable population. The Deschutes National Forest has closed perimeter ditches at Big Marsh, where past drainage and grazing had led to degradation of the marsh. The Mt. Hood National Forest has fenced sections of Camas Prairie and restricted excessive grazing of the meadow. Implementation of these conservation actions is expected to improve breeding success of Oregon spotted frogs at these locations, but data confirming this hypothesis are not yet available. In addition, BLM's Prineville District Office recently completed encroachment removal projects and repairs to headcuts in systems that have had historically or currently have Oregon spotted frogs. Headcutting is a process of active erosion in a channel caused by an abrupt change in slope. Turbulence in the water undercuts substrate material resulting in collapse of the upper level. This under-cut-collapse process advances up the stream channel. The results of BLM's efforts are unknown at this time; however, they were completed specifically to ameliorate threats to Oregon spotted frog habitat.

Since 1994, in the Oregon portion of the Klamath Basin, the Service's Partners for Fish and Wildlife Program, in collaboration with private landowners, has restored approximately 8,832 ac (3,568 ha) of wetlands adjacent to Upper Klamath Lake. Several habitat restoration projects are underway in known occupied areas including Crane Creek, Sevenmile Creek, Jack Creek, and the Upper Williamson River. Restoration projects include re-channelizing creeks and rivers to provide breeding and rearing habitat, construction of breeding ponds, construction of riparian fences to exclude cattle, and the installation of alternate water sources. To date, Oregon spotted frogs have been detected in only one restored, previously unoccupied wetland area, although survey efforts in restored habitats have not yet been completed.

The BLM's Klamath Falls Field Office has initiated several habitat restoration projects within their Wood River Wetland property, including installation of water control structures, construction of breeding ponds, and canal restructuring for additional breeding areas. To date, 3,000 ac (1,214 ha) of wetland habitats associated with the Wood River Canal have been restored. However, for reasons unknown, Oregon spotted frogs have not been detected in the restored wetlands, but rather have only been associated with the canal system (BLM multiple data sources). BLM actively manages the water in the canal during the breeding season to prevent stranding and inundating

Oregon spotted frog egg masses.

The Fremont-Winema National Forest, Chemult Ranger District, in the Oregon portion of the Klamath Basin has initiated a project to restore habitat along Jack Creek, which as of 2008, includes the removal of cattle from a portion of the lands owned by the USFS (Gervais 2011 p. 9). In addition, encroaching lodgepole pine (Gervais 2011 pp. 11-12) has been thinned on both USFS and private lands as a result of this project. In cooperation with adjacent private landowners, the USFS recently released seven beavers into the Jack Creek watershed (Simpson 2012, pers. comm.), which is intended to increase the open water and breeding habitat for Oregon spotted frogs. One of the private landowners has also installed log fences to protect three Oregon spotted frog pools, and two off-stream water sources to exclude cattle from riparian areas, and wattle installment (a fabrication of poles interwoven with slender branches) for water retention (Markus 2012, pers. comm.). In addition, in 2009, the USFS installed fences at Buck Meadow to control grazing on the USFS lands (Lerum 2012, p. 18). The long-term benefits of the USFS efforts are unknown at this time; however, these actions were completed to specifically ameliorate threats to the Oregon spotted frog's habitat.

The USFS has completed and continues to work on Oregon spotted frog site management plans that identify threats and management actions to reduce threats at each of the following sites: Sevenmile, Jack Creek, Buck Lake, Dilman Meadow, Hosmer Lake, Lava and Little Lava Lake, Big Marsh, Odell/Davis Lake, Little Cultus Lake, Mink Lake Basin, and Gold Lake. Implementation of management actions is voluntary and dependent upon funding, and will likely occur at the District level.

The comprehensive conservation plan (CCP) for Klamath Marsh NWR includes conservation actions for maintaining or improving local habitat conditions for the benefit of Oregon spotted frogs on NWR property. These include: Restoring or maintaining hydrologic regimes, protecting and restoring ephemeral and permanent wetlands, restoring or maintaining open water and early seral vegetation communities, reevaluating or discontinuing fish stocking practices, developing comprehensive grazing strategies or adaptive management plans where livestock occur in habitat, and working locally and cooperatively to maintain and restore habitat conditions and to monitor the outcomes of management actions for Oregon spotted frog (USFWS 2010a, p. 72). The CCPs detail program planning levels that are sometimes substantially above current budget allocations and are primarily used for strategic planning and priority setting; thus inclusion of a project in a CCP does not guarantee that the project will be implemented. However, implementation of the above conservation actions within the CCP could benefit a minimum of 338 breeding individuals. These actions are expected to improve the status of the Oregon spotted frog on the Klamath Marsh NWR if adequate budget allocations are provided and the projects are implemented. Existing wetland restoration activities at Klamath Marsh NWR have been limited to invasive weed management (Mauser 2012, pers. comm.).

Summary of habitat or range destruction, modification, or curtailment— Past human actions have destroyed, modified, and curtailed the range and habitat available for the Oregon spotted frog, which is now absent from an estimated 76 to 90 percent of its former range. The loss of wetlands is continuing at certain locations in at least 10 of the 15 remaining occupied sub-basins, particularly on private lands. The historical and ongoing alteration of hydrological processes resulting from the operation of existing water diversions/manipulation structures, existing and new roads, residential development, agricultural areas, and the removal of beavers continues to impact Oregon spotted frogs and their habitat. The changes in hydrology result in the loss of breeding through inundation or desiccation of egg masses, loss or degradation of habitat necessary for all Oregon spotted frog life stages, and the creation of habitat conditions that support nonnative predaceous species.

Reed canarygrass invasions, plant succession, and restoration plantings continue to modify and reduce the amount and quality of habitat necessary for all Oregon spotted frog life stages. The timing and intensity of livestock grazing, or lack thereof, continues to change the quality of Oregon spotted frog habitat in British Columbia, Washington, and Oregon due to increased sedimentation, increased water temperatures, and reduced water quality. Oregon spotted frogs in all currently occupied sub-basins are subject to one or more of these threats to their habitat. Eleven of the 15 occupied sub-basins are currently experiencing a high to very high level of impact, primarily due to hydrological changes/manipulations, vegetation encroachment, and reed canarygrass invasions. These impacts are ongoing, are expected to continue into the future, and affect habitat that supports all life stages of the Oregon spotted frog.

The benefits of the conservation actions to Oregon spotted frogs are site-specific, but are not sufficient to ameliorate the habitat threats at a sub-basin scale. Wetland restoration efforts have been implemented, but rarely are these specifically designed for Oregon spotted frogs, and may inadvertently reduce habitat quality for this emergent wetland-dependent species. Further, post-restoration monitoring has not been accomplished to evaluate whether these efforts are benefiting Oregon spotted frogs. Therefore, based on the best information available, the threats to Oregon spotted frog from habitat destruction, modification, or curtailment are occurring throughout the entire range of the species, and are expected to continue into the future.

Factor B. Overutilization for Commercial, Recreational, Scientific, or Educational Purposes

Overutilization for commercial, recreational, scientific, or educational purposes has been documented for a wide range of amphibians. During the egg-laying period, Oregon spotted frogs occur in relatively easy-to-access locations that could make them easy to collect. However, we are not aware of collection of Oregon spotted frogs for commercial, recreational, or educational purposes.

Oregon spotted frog populations may be negatively impacted by scientific studies. In all Washington breeding locations and some of the breeding locations in British Columbia and Oregon, surveys are conducted annually during the egg-laying period. While these surveys are conducted in a manner to avoid trampling of frogs and egg masses (protocol example Pearl et al. 2010), such impacts may still occur. The extent to which any population is impacted by these surveys is unknown, but expected to be low. Eggs were collected each year beginning in 2002 from at least two of the extant locations in British Columbia for a headstart rearing program, which released metamorphic Oregon spotted frogs back into those sites (COSFRT 2012, pp. 30-31). This effort has ceased because it was deemed unsuccessful at bolstering the extant populations; however, captive husbandry for potential release into new locations continues.

The WDFW has collected 7,870 eggs (through 2011) from various breeding locations on the Black River and Conboy Lake NWRs for their captive-rearing program (Tirhi and Schmidt 2011, pp. 51-55). During this period, the population has continued to decline at Conboy Lake, but the source of the decline is unclear and cannot specifically be attributed to the egg collection. The USGS and Colorado State University have been collecting eggs in the Deschutes and Klamath Basins for genetic studies since 2007, resulting in the collection of at least 3,000 eggs (Robertson and Funk 2012 pp. 8-11; Pearl 2012, pers. comm.). However, we have no evidence to indicate that Oregon spotted frogs are being overutilized for commercial, recreational, scientific, or educational purposes such that this activity currently poses a threat to the species or is likely to in the future.

Factor C. Disease or Predation

Disease

Amphibians are affected by a variety of diseases, and some diseases are known to negatively affect declining amphibian species. Diseases that are currently known to occur in Oregon spotted frogs and have the potential to affect populations are briefly discussed below. The specific effects of disease and parasitism on Oregon spotted frogs are not well documented.

Red-Leg Syndrome— Red-leg syndrome has been identified in several declining amphibian species but is not known to be a significant problem for the Oregon spotted frog (Blaustein 1999, pers. comm.). Red-leg syndrome refers to a common condition in which there is a reddening of the lower body, usually the legs and sometimes the abdomen, due to a dilation of capillaries under the skin. This disease is presumed to be widespread, having been reported for >100 years in many different species of frogs and salamanders in captivity and in the wild (Densmore and Green 2007, p. 236).

Chytrid Fungus—Bd has been implicated in the decline and extinction of numerous amphibian species in multiple locations around the world (Speare and Berger 2004). In the United States, 7 families including 18 amphibian species have been diagnosed as infected with Bd (Speare and Berger 2004). Bd infection has been documented in at least seven ranid frog species from the PNW, including Oregon spotted frogs (Adams et al. 2010, p. 295; Pearl et al. 2009b, p. 212; Hayes et al. 2009, p. 149). Chytridiomycosis is a cutaneous infection that "results in a severe diffuse dermatitis characterized by epidermal hyperplasia, hyperkeratosis, and variable degrees of cutaneous ulceration and hyperemia" (Bradley et al. 2002, p. 206). Clinical signs can include lethargy, abnormal posture, loss of the righting reflex (ability to turn over), and death (Daszak et al. 1999, p. 737). The fungal organism, Bd, is likely transmitted by release of zoospores into the water that eventually contact a susceptible animal, penetrating the skin, and establishing an infection (Pessier et al. 1999, p. 198; Bradley et al. 2002, p. 206). Dermal infections by Bd are thought to cause mortality by interfering with skin functions, including maintaining fluid and electrolyte homeostasis (balance), respiration, and the skin's role as a barrier to toxic and infectious agents (Pessier et al. 1999, p. 198; Bradley et al. 2002, p. 206). Unlike most other vertebrates, amphibians drink water and absorb important salts (electrolytes) through the skin rather than the mouth. In diseased individuals, electrolyte transport across the epidermis was inhibited by >50 percent, resulting in cardiac arrest and death (Voyles et al. 2009, pp. 582, 585).

In 2007 and 2008, the USGS sampled Oregon spotted frogs at sites across Washington and Oregon; Bd was confirmed at all locations sampled (Pearl et al. 2009b, p. 212). Even though Pearl et al. (2009b, p. 216) detected Bd at 100 percent of the sites sampled, they did not observe morbidity or mortality that could be attributed to chytridiomycosis. In addition to confirmation at USGS-sampled sites, Bd has been confirmed in Oregon spotted frogs near Sunriver in central Oregon (Bowerman 2005, pers. comm.) and Conboy Lake NWR (Hayes et al. 2009, p. 149) in Washington. Pearl et al. (2007, p. 147) detected Bd more frequently in highly aquatic species, such as Oregon spotted frogs, than in species with more terrestrial adult stages and shorter larval periods, suggesting that Oregon spotted frogs may be experiencing elevated exposure and infection due to their highly aquatic life-history. In addition, modeling done by Pearl et al. (2009b, p. 213) indicates that juvenile Oregon spotted frogs that test positive for Bd infection are more likely to have a poorer body condition after overwintering than individuals that test negative for Bd infection.

Alone, Bd may not be a concern for some healthy amphibian populations; however, most of the

Oregon spotted frog populations in Oregon and Washington are already exposed to several stressors, such as predation, competition from nonnative species, and water quality degradation, and the effects of Bd are likely to be exacerbated and potentially compounded by these interactions (for example, see Parris and Baud 2004, pp. 346-347; Parris and Cornelius 2004, pp. 3388-3390; Parris and Beaudoin 2004, p. 628). In addition, Bd has been found in nonnative species that co-occur with Oregon spotted frogs in central Oregon (Pearl et al. 2007, p. 147); in particular, bullfrogs may serve as a Bd host while experiencing limited negative effects from the pathogen (Daszak et al. 2004, p. 203).

Laboratory studies have shown that infecting Oregon spotted frogs with Bd inhibits growth without necessarily showing any direct clinical signs (Padgett-Flohr and Hayes 2011). Recently metamorphosed frogs exposed to one of two strains of Bd tested positive for the pathogen within 11 days after exposure; however, no frogs died or displayed clinical signs of disease and most (83 percent) tested negative for the pathogen within 90 days of exposure. However, infected frogs gained significantly less weight than control animals, suggesting the infection carried an energetic cost. The detection of Bd at all Oregon spotted frog sites sampled, combined with the lack of observed mortality (in the wild and laboratory testing), indicates Oregon spotted frogs may be able to persist with Bd infections (Pearl et al. 2009b, p. 216) but growth and presumed long-term survival (e.g., avoidance of predators) are inhibited. Consequently, in light of the numerous amphibian extinctions attributed to Bd, and in conjunction with the other stressors that impact Oregon spotted frogs, we conclude that Bd poses a risk to individual Oregon spotted frog populations, particularly those most susceptible to climate changes (see Factor E discussion), but additional studies are necessary to determine whether Bd is a threat rangewide to the Oregon spotted frog.

Other pathogens, such as iridoviruses (specifically Ranavirus), have been documented to cause mortality in North American amphibians (Dasak et al. 1999, pp. 741-743). While not yet documented in wild Oregon spotted frog populations, iridovirus outbreaks have been identified as a major source of mortality in British Columbia captive-rearing programs for Oregon spotted frogs (COSEWIC 2011, p. 35).

Saprolegnia—The oomycete water mold Saprolegnia has been suggested as one of the causes of amphibian declines in the PNW (Kiesecker and Blaustein 1997, p. 218). Genetic analysis confirmed oomycetes of multiple genera on amphibian eggs in the PNW, including Oregon spotted frogs (Petrisko et al. 2008, pp. 174-178). McAllister and Leonard (1997, p. 25) reported destruction of developing Oregon spotted frog egg masses by this fungus, but not to the extent observed in other amphibian eggs. The threat of Saprolegnia to Oregon spotted frog populations is unclear, but this fungus has been shown to destroy Oregon spotted frog egg masses and could pose a threat to individual Oregon spotted frog breeding areas in the future.

Ultraviolet-B Radiation—Impacts resulting from exposure to ultraviolet-B (UV-B) radiation appear to vary greatly between amphibian species. Ambient levels of UV-B radiation in the atmosphere have risen significantly over the past few decades due to decreases in stratospheric ozone, climate warming, and lake acidification. Because amphibian eggs lack shells and adults and tadpoles have thin, delicate skin, they are extremely vulnerable to increased levels of UV-B radiation. However, the harmful effects of UV-B radiation on amphibians depend upon a number of variables (Blaustein et al. 2003, pp. 123-128). Studies summarized in Blaustein et al. (2003) indicate UV-B exposure can result in mortality, as well as a variety of sublethal effects, including behavior alteration, slow growth and development, and developmental and physiological malformations. The type and severity of effect varies by life stage exposed and dosage of UV-B. Experimental tests conducted by Blaustein et al. (1999, p. 1102) found the hatching success of Oregon spotted frogs was unaffected by UV-B, indicating their eggs may be UV-resistant. However, a meta-analysis of available published literature conducted by Bancroft et al. (2008)

found that exposure to UV-B resulted in a 1.9-fold reduction in amphibian survival and that larvae (tadpoles) were more susceptible than embryos. In addition, Bancroft et al. (2008) determined that UV-B interacted synergistically with other environmental stressors, such as contaminants, resulting in greater than additive effects on survival. For example, Kiesecker and Blaustein (1997, pp. 217-218) found increased mortality associated with the fungus identified as Saprolegnia ferax in amphibian embryos exposed to UV-B; especially susceptible were amphibians that lay eggs in communal egg masses, like Oregon spotted frogs. At present, the extent of population-level impacts from UV-B exposure is unknown.

Malformations—The North American Reporting Center for Amphibian Malformations (NBII 2005) documents amphibian malformations throughout the United States. Malformations of several Rana species, including the Cascades frog (Rana cascadae), red-legged frog (Rana aurora), foothill yellow-legged frog (Rana boylii), and bullfrog, have been reported within the current and historical range of the Oregon spotted frog in Washington, Oregon, and California. We are aware of one report from Thurston County, Washington, of an Oregon spotted frog with an extra forelimb (NBII 2005) and reports of malformations from Deschutes (Johnson et al. 2002a, p. 157; Bowerman and Johnson 2003, pp. 142-144), Douglas, and Lane (NBII 2005) Counties in Oregon. Based on research on numerous amphibian species, including Oregon spotted frog, growing evidence suggests that the high frequencies of severe limb malformations may be caused by a parasitic infection (Ribeiroia ondatrae) in amphibian larvae (Johnson et al. 2002a, p. 162). Recent investigations also indicate small fish and certain libellulid and corduliid dragonfly larvae attack developing tadpoles and can cause high incidences of missing-limb deformities, including complete amputation (Ballengee and Sessions 2009; Bowerman et al. 2010). At present, the extent of population-level impacts from malformations among Oregon spotted frogs is unknown.

Parasitic infection—Aquatic snails (Planorbella spp.) are the exclusive intermediate host for the trematode Ribeiroia ondatrae (Johnson and Chase 2004, p. 523) and are found in a diversity of habitats, including ephemeral ponds, montane lakes, stock ponds, oxbows, drainage canals, and reservoirs (Johnson et al. 2002a, p. 164). Trematodes are parasitic flatworms that have a thick outer cuticle and one or more suckers or hooks for attaching to host tissue. Johnson et al. (2002a, p. 165) postulate that the dramatic and widespread alterations of aquatic ecosystems, particularly the construction of small impoundments or farm ponds, may have created environments that facilitate high densities of Planorbella snails and the resulting infections from R. ondatrae. Many of the sites with high frequencies of malformations were impacted heavily by cattle and supported dense Planorbella snail populations. Malformations in multiple amphibian species were found in Washington ponds that had a history of grazing that extended back at least 50 years (Johnson et al. 2002a, p. 165).

Johnson et al. (2002a, p. 166) found the frequency of malformations in larval amphibians was significantly higher than in transformed amphibians from the same system, suggesting that malformed larvae experience greater mortality prior to and during metamorphosis. However, sensitivity to and severity (mortality versus no malformation) of infection varies by amphibian species (Johnson and Hartson 2009, p. 195) and tadpole stage exposed (Schotthoefer et al. 2003, p. 1148).

High levels of R. ondatrae infection and the resulting malformations may increase mortality in wild amphibian populations and may represent a threat to amphibian populations already in decline. Johnson et al. (2002a, p. 157) and Bowerman and Johnson (2003, pp. 142-144) have found deformities in Oregon spotted frogs caused by this parasite at the Sunriver Nature Center Pond, which had a high population of large planorbid snails. Three additional ponds within 6 mi (10 km) were also investigated, each of which supported planorbid snails, but at lower infestation levels. None of these ponds yielded malformed Oregon spotted frogs (Bowerman et al. 2003, pp. 142-143). Most of the malformations found in anuran frogs were around the hind limbs, where they are more likely to be debilitating (hinder mobility) and expose the frog to increased risk of predation (reduced escape/evade ability) (Johnson et al. 2002a, p. 162). In a study on wood frogs (Rana sylvatica), Michel and Burke (2011) reported malformed tadpoles were twice as vulnerable to predators because they could not escape or evade.

Human manipulation of upland areas adjacent to amphibian breeding areas and direct manipulation of the breeding areas can affect the prevalence of Planorbella snails and the infection rate of R. ondatrae. Complex habitats reduce transmission rates of larval trematodes because these habitats provide more refugia for tadpoles. Alternatively, simplified habitats, such as agricultural landscapes, have been shown to reduce parasite prevalence by limiting access of vertebrate hosts, particularly in birds (King et al. 2007, p. 2074). However, when simplified habitats are subject to water runoff associated with agricultural, cattle, or urban sources and eutrophication, the abundance of snails can increase, thereby increasing the prevalence of trematodes and parasitic risks to frogs (Johnson and Chase 2004, pp. 522-523; Johnson et al. 2007 p. 15782). While the effects of these parasite-induced malformations are clear at the individual scale, population-level effects remain largely uninvestigated. However, Biek et al. (2002, p. 731) found that the viabilities of pond-breeding amphibians were most vulnerable to reductions in juvenile or adult survival relative to other portions of the life cycles. Therefore, it is reasonable to infer that where Planorbella snails coincide with Oregon spotted frogs, malformations will occur resulting in mortality of juvenile frogs and a reduction in the viability of the Oregon spotted frog population at that location. At present, it is not known where these co-occurrences take place, or how extensive infections levels may be, but 11 of the occupied sub-basins have agricultural, cattle, or urban sources that produce runoff that can increase the snail populations and negative effects have been demonstrated at the Sunriver Nature Center Pond population.

Predation

Predation is a process of major importance in influencing the distribution, abundance, and diversity of species in ecological communities. Generally, predation leads to changes in both the population size of the predator and that of the prey. In unfavorable environments, prey species are stressed or living at low population densities such that predation is likely to have negative effects on all prey species, thus lowering species richness. In addition, when a nonnative predator is introduced to the ecosystem, negative effects on the prey population may be higher than those from co-evolved native predators. The effects of predation may be magnified when populations are small, and the disproportionate effect of predation on declining populations has been shown to drive rare species even further toward extinction (Woodworth 1999, pp. 74-75).

Introduced fish species within the historical range of the Oregon spotted frog may have contributed to losses of populations. Oregon spotted frogs, which are palatable to fish, did not evolve with these introduced species and may not have the mechanisms to avoid the predatory fish that prey on the tadpoles. The microhabitat requirement of the Oregon spotted frog, unique among native ranids of the PNW, exposes it to a number of introduced fish species (Hayes 1994, p. 25), such as smallmouth bass (Micropterus dolomieu), largemouth bass (Micropterus salmoides), pumpkinseed (Lepomis gibbosus), yellow perch (Perca flavescens), bluegill (Lepomis macrochirus), brown bullhead (Ameriurus nebulosus), black crappie (Pomoxis nigromaculatus), warmouth (Lepomis gulosus), brook trout (Salvelinus fontinalis), rainbow trout (Oncorhynchus mykiss), fathead minnow (Pimephales promelas) (Hayes and Jennings 1986, pp. 494-496; Hayes 1997, pp. 42-43; Hayes et al. 1997; McAllister and Leonard 1997, p. 14; Engler 1999, pers. comm.), and mosquitofish (Gambusia affinis) (Wydoski and Whitney 2003, p. 163; Johnson 2008, p. 5).

Surveys from 1993 to 1997 in British Columbia, Washington, and Oregon documented at least one introduced predator in 20 of 24 sites (Hayes et al. 1997, p. 5). Brook trout was the most frequently recorded introduced predator, which was recorded at 18 of 24 sites. Although differences in temperature requirements between the two species may limit their interactions, brook trout apparently occur with the Oregon spotted frog at cold-water springs, where the latter species probably overwinters and where cooler water is favorable to brook trout (Hayes et al. 1997, p. 5). During drought years, dropping water levels result in overlap in habitat use between these two species. As wetland refuges are reduced, Oregon spotted frogs become concentrated and the larval stages are exposed to brook trout predation (Hayes et al. 1997, p. 5; Hayes 1998a, p. 15), resulting in lower Oregon spotted frog recruitment (Pearl 1999, p. 18). In addition to effects in breeding habitat, Pearl et al. (2009a, p. 143) found substantial evidence for a negative effect on overwintering Oregon spotted frogs from nonnative fish with access to spring and channel habitats. In these latter situations, predation is believed to be more pronounced in spatially constrained overwintering habitats where frogs and fish may both seek flowing water with dissolved oxygen. Their findings suggest that these negative effects are mediated by habitat complexity and the seasonal use of microhabitats, and Oregon spotted frogs can benefit from fish-free overwintering sites, even if fish are present in other local habitats.

Demographic data indicate that sites with significant numbers of brook trout and/or fathead minnow have a skewed ratio of older spotted frogs to juvenile frogs, suggesting poor reproductive success or juvenile recruitment (Hayes 1997, pp. 42-43, 1998a). While experimental data are sparse, field surveys involving other western amphibians (e.g., Adams 1999, p. 1168; Monello and Wright 1999, pp. 299-300; Bull and Marx 2002, pp. 245-247; Vredenberg 2004; Knapp 2005, pp. 275-276; Pearl et al. 2005b, pp. 82-83; Rowe and Garcia 2014, pp. 146-147) and other closely related frog species strongly suggest that introduced fish represent a threat to Oregon spotted frogs that has significant impacts (Pearl 1999, pp. 17-18). A study of the impacts of introduced trout on Columbia spotted frog populations in Idaho revealed that, although fish and adult frogs coexisted at many of the stocked lakes, most stocked lakes contained significantly lower densities of all amphibian life stages (Pilliod and Peterson 2001, p. 326). On the other hand, results from the Willamette Valley in Oregon suggest that nonnative, warm water fishes actually benefit introduced populations of bullfrogs because of fish predation on macroinvertebrates that would otherwise prey on bullfrog larvae (Adams et al. 2003, p. 347).

The presence of these nonnative species has been shown to increase the time for metamorphosis and decrease the mass of native red-legged frogs (Kiesecker and Blaustein 1997; Lawler et al. 1999, p. 617). A recent study documented nonnative fish negatively influencing the survival and growth of Pacific tree frogs while bullfrog larvae reduced the growth but had no effect on survival (Preston et al. 2012, p. 1257). In addition, the predation effects of nonnative fish and bullfrogs on Pacific tree frogs were additive, but those species had little impact on each other (Preston et al. 2012, p. 1259). Many of the sub-basins occupied by Oregon spotted frogs also have introduced warm- and/or cold-water fish, and 5 of the 15 sub-basins are subject to high to very high impacts due to predation of larvae and reduced winter survival.

The ODFW stocks fish in most of the Cascades Lakes and two reservoirs in the Upper Deschutes River sub-basin occupied by Oregon spotted frogs (Hodgson 2012, pers. comm.). In addition to stocking, there is natural production of various fish species, both native and introduced, in the lakes and reservoirs in the Upper Deschutes River sub-basin and in lakes in the McKenzie River and Middle Fork Willamette sub-basins where spotted frogs occur (Hodgson 2012, pers. comm.; Ziller 2013, pers. comm.; USFS 2011a). The ODFW no longer stocks fish in any of the moving waters associated with Oregon spotted frog locations within the Klamath Basin (Tinniswood 2012, pers. comm.).

Bullfrogs introduced from eastern North America into the historical range of the Oregon spotted frog may have contributed to losses of populations. The introduction of bullfrogs may have played a role in the disappearance of Oregon spotted frogs from the Willamette Valley in Oregon and the Puget Sound area in Washington (Nussbaum et al. 1983, p. 187). Bullfrogs share similar habitat and temperature requirements with the Oregon spotted frog, and the overlap in time and space between the two species is believed to be extensive (Hayes 1994, p. 25; Hayes et al. 1997, p. 5). Bullfrogs can reach high densities due to the production of large numbers of eggs per breeding female and unpalatability (and high survivorship) of tadpoles to predatory fish (Kruse and Francis 1977, pp. 250-251). Bullfrog tadpoles outcompete or displace tadpoles of native frog species from their habitat or optimal conditions (Kupferberg 1997, pp. 1741-1746; Kiesecker and Blaustein 1998, pp. 783-784; Kiesecker et al. 2001b, pp. 1966-1967).

Bullfrog adults achieve larger size than native western ranids and even juvenile bullfrogs can consume native frogs (Hayes and Jennings 1986, p. 492; Pearl et al. 2004, p. 16). The digestive tracts of a sample of 25 adult bullfrogs from Conboy Lake in Washington contained nine Oregon spotted frogs, including seven adults (McAllister and Leonard 1997, p. 13). A later examination of the stomachs of two large bullfrogs revealed two adult or subadult Oregon spotted frogs in one stomach and four in the second (Hayes 1999, pers. comm.). Bullfrogs were recorded consuming hatchling Oregon spotted frogs at British Columbia's Maintenance Detachment Aldergrove site (Haycock and Woods 2001, unpubl. data cited in COSFRT 2012, p. 19). In addition, the USGS has observed Oregon spotted frogs within dissected bullfrogs at multiple sites throughout the Deschutes and Klamath Basins (Pearl 2012, pers comm.).

Oregon spotted frogs are more susceptible to predation by bullfrogs than are northern red-legged frogs (Pearl et al. 2004, p. 16). Oregon spotted frogs and northern red-legged frogs historically coexisted in areas of the PNW that are now invaded by bullfrogs. However, the Oregon spotted frog has declined more severely than the northern red-legged frog. Pearl et al. (2004, p. 16) demonstrated in laboratory experiments that the more aquatic Oregon spotted frog juveniles are consumed by bullfrogs at a higher rate than are northern red-legged frog juveniles. Oregon spotted frogs and northern red-legged frogs also differ in their ability to escape bullfrogs, with Oregon spotted frogs having shorter mean and maximum jump distances than northern red-legged frogs of equal size. Bullfrogs, therefore, pose a greater threat to Oregon spotted frogs than to red-legged frogs. Oregon spotted frog's microhabitat use and escape abilities may be limiting their distributions in historical lowland habitats where bullfrogs are present, whereas red-legged frog populations are more stable (Pearl et al. 2004, pp. 17-18).

The ability of bullfrogs and Oregon spotted frogs to coexist may be related to differences in seasonal and permanent wetland use. However, a substantial bullfrog population has likely coexisted with Oregon spotted frogs for nearly 50 years in Conboy Lake in Washington (Rombough et al. 2006, p. 210). This long-term overlap has been hypothesized to be the evolutionary driver for larger body size of Oregon spotted frogs at Conboy Lake (Rombough et al. 2006, p. 210). However, body size measurements have not been completed across the range for a complete comparison to be made. Winterkill could be a factor in controlling the bullfrog population at Conboy Lake and, hence, facilitating co-existence with Oregon spotted frogs (Engler and Hayes 1998, p. 2); however, the Oregon spotted frog population at Conboy Lake has declined over the last decade, some of which is likely due to bullfrog predation. Bullfrogs have been actively managed in the Sunriver area in Oregon for more than 40 years, and despite efforts to eradicate them, they have been expanding in distribution (Bowerman 2012, pers. comm.). Bullfrogs have been documented up to 4,300 feet (1,311 m) elevation in the Little Deschutes River sub-basin in habitat occupied by Oregon spotted frog. Bullfrogs have been found in 10 of the 15 sub-basins occupied by Oregon spotted frogs, but are relatively rare at most of the locations where they co-occur. However, based on our threats analysis, the impacts due to predation and/or competition with bullfrogs within the Lower Fraser River, Middle Klickitat sub-basins in Washington, and the Upper Klamath Lake sub-basin in Oregon are considered to be high to very high because of the more extensive overlap between these two species in these areas.

Green frogs (Lithobates clamitans) are native to the eastern United States but have been introduced to the western United States and Canada. This introduced species occurs at a few lakes in Whatcom County, Washington (McAllister 1995; WDFW WSDM database), but Oregon spotted frogs are not known to occur in these lakes. Green frogs do co-occur with Oregon spotted frogs at Maria and Mountain Sloughs in British Columbia (COSEWIC 2011, p. 36). Adult green frogs may eat young Oregon spotted frogs, but adult Oregon spotted frogs may reach a size that is too large to be prey for the species. Whether green frogs are significant competitors of Oregon spotted frogs is currently unknown. High population densities of green frogs possibly attract and maintain higher than normal population densities of native predators, which in turn increases predation pressure on Oregon spotted frogs (COSFRT 2012, p. 19).

Conservation Efforts To Reduce Disease or Predation

Despite considerable knowledge about the habitat and management requirements for Oregon spotted frog, refuge management at the Conboy Lake NWR remains complex as habitat needs and the abatement of other stressors often conflict with the conventional intensive wetland management that occurs on the refuge (USFWS, 2010b, p. 64). The historical Conboy Lake basin in Washington likely retained water for 10 to 12 months in most years. Currently, it retains water only during wet years and is drained annually by the Conboy Lake NWR to control bullfrogs for the benefit of Oregon spotted frogs. However, the draining of the lakebed forces all surviving bullfrogs, fish, and Oregon spotted frogs into the canal system for the fall and winter, increasing potential predation on Oregon spotted frogs.

In the Upper and Little Deschutes River sub-basins in Oregon, there has been little effort to control invasive predators. Bullfrog eradication has been attempted at two sites within the Upper and Little Deschutes sub-basins: Sunriver and Crosswater, respectively. However, it appears that bullfrogs may be increasing in the Sunriver area (Bowerman 2012, pers. comm.).

Current predator or disease conservation efforts in the Klamath Basin in Oregon are limited to bullfrog control or eradication. The USGS has conducted a bullfrog eradication program on Crane Creek since bullfrogs appeared in 2010. In addition, the BLM has been controlling and reducing bullfrogs and analyzing the gut contents of bullfrogs at all life stages on their Wood River property in Oregon for 6 years. Bullfrog detections and collection have decreased in different areas of the canal in recent years (Roninger 2012, pers. comm.). The number of bullfrogs removed and seen at this site has decreased, and in the last few years, the bulk of the bullfrog removal has been from the north canal and Seven-mile canal areas (outside the Oregon spotted frog site), which is considered to be the strongest source areas for movement into the Oregon spotted frog site (Roninger 2012, pers. comm). However, despite these efforts, bullfrogs continue to persist in these Oregon spotted frog habitats.

Summary of disease and predation—Saprolegnia, Bd, and Ribeiroia ondatrae have been found in Oregon spotted frogs and compounded with other stressors, such as UV-B exposure, degradation of habitat quality, or increased predation pressure, may contribute to population declines. Bd and R. ondatrae, in particular, infect post-metamorphic frogs and reductions in these life stages are more likely to lead to population declines in pond-breeding amphibians; however, these are not currently known to be causing population declines in Oregon spotted frogs. Disease continues to be a concern, but more information is needed to determine the severity of impact that diseases may have on Oregon spotted frogs. Therefore, based on the best available scientific evidence, there is no indication that disease is a threat to the Oregon spotted frog.

Introduced fish species prey on tadpoles, negatively affect overwintering habitat, and can significantly threaten Oregon spotted frog populations, especially during droughts, as aquatic habitat areas become smaller and escape cover is reduced. Cushman et al. 2007 (p. 22) states that both Hayes (1997) and Pearl (1999) hypothesized that low water conditions have the potential to increase overlap between Oregon spotted frog and nonnative predators such as brook trout and bullfrogs. Increased overlap in habitat use between Oregon spotted frog and nonnative predators is likely to result in greater loss to predation. Bullfrogs (and likely green frogs) prey on juvenile and adult Oregon spotted frogs and bullfrog larvae can outcompete or displace Oregon spotted frog larvae, effectively reducing all Oregon spotted frog life stages and posing a significant threat to Oregon spotted frogs. At least one nonnative predaceous species occurs within each of the sub-basins currently occupied by Oregon spotted frogs, and most sub-basins have multiple predators. Nine of the 15 occupied sub-basins are currently experiencing moderate to very high impacts due to predation, and threats from predators are more concentrated in summer/rearing and overwintering habitat. While some predator control occurs in a few sub-basins, this work is not sufficient to ameliorate the threat from predators.

Therefore, based on our review of the best information available, we conclude that predation is a threat to Oregon spotted frogs throughout the entire range of the species and is expected to continue into the future.

Factor D. The Inadequacy of Existing Regulatory Mechanisms

Under this factor, we examine whether existing regulatory mechanisms are inadequate to address the threats to the species discussed under the other factors. Section 4(b)(1)(A) of the Act requires the Service to take into account "those efforts, if any, being made by any State or foreign nation, or any political subdivision of a State or foreign nation, to protect such specie. . . ." In relation to Factor D under the Act, we interpret this language to require the Service to consider relevant Federal, State, and tribal laws, regulations, and other such mechanisms that may minimize any of the threats we describe in threat analyses under the other four factors, or otherwise enhance conservation of the species. We give strongest weight to statutes and their implementing regulations and to management direction that stems from those laws and regulations. An example would be State governmental actions enforced under a State statute or constitution, or Federal action under statute.

Having evaluated the significance of the threat as mitigated by any such conservation efforts, we analyze under Factor D the extent to which existing regulatory mechanisms are inadequate to address the specific threats to the species. Regulatory mechanisms, if they exist, may reduce or eliminate the impacts from one or more identified threats. In this section, we review existing State and Federal regulatory mechanisms to determine whether they effectively reduce or remove threats to the Oregon spotted frog.

Canadian Laws and Regulations

In Canada, few regulatory mechanisms protect or conserve Oregon spotted frogs. In British Columbia, Oregon spotted frogs are on the Conservation Data Centre's Red List. The Red List includes ecological communities, indigenous species and subspecies that are extirpated, endangered, or threatened in British Columbia; placing taxa on the Red List flags them as being at risk and requiring investigation, but does not confer any protection (British Columbia Ministry of Environment 2012, p. 1).

The Oregon spotted frog was determined to be endangered by the Committee on the Status of Endangered Wildlife in Canada in 1999, with status reexamined and confirmed in 2000 and 2011, and it received an endangered determination under the Canadian Species at Risk Act (SARA) in 2003 (COSFRT 2012, p. 1). SARA makes it an offense to kill, harm, harass, capture or take an individual of a listed species that is extirpated, endangered or threatened; or to possess, collect, buy, sell or trade an individual of a listed species that is extirpated, endangered or threatened, or any part or derivative of such an individual (S.C. ch. 29 section 32); or damage or destroy the residence of one or more individuals of a listed endangered or threatened species or of a listed extirpated species if a recovery strategy has recommended its reintroduction (S.C. ch, 29 sections 33, 58). For species other than birds, the prohibitions on harm to individuals and destruction of residences are limited to Federal lands. Three of the four breeding locations in Canada occur wholly or partially on private lands, which are not subject to SARA prohibitions (COSEWIC 2011, p. 38).

Habitat protection in British Columbia is limited to the Federal Fisheries Act, British Columbia Water Act, and the provincial Riparian Areas Regulation (COSEWIC 2011, p. 38). The Federal Fisheries Act limits activities that can cause harmful alteration, disruption, or destruction of fish habitat, with the primary goal being no net loss of fish habitat. The British Columbia Water Act is the principal law for managing the diversion and use of provincial water resources. License holders are entitled to divert and use water; store water; construct, maintain, and operate anything capable of or used for the proper diversion, storage, carriage, distribution, and use of the water or the power produced from it; alter or improve a stream or channel for any purpose; and construct fences, screens, and fish or game guards across streams for the purpose of conserving fish and wildlife (British Columbia Water Act Part 2, section 5). The Riparian Areas Regulation was enacted under Section 12 of the Fish Protection Act and calls on local governments to protect riparian fish habitat during residential, commercial, and industrial development. The habitat protections under these Canadian Acts are designed to benefit fish species. As discussed under Factor A, riparian protection and restoration actions designed specifically to benefit fish can be detrimental to Oregon spotted frogs and their habitat.

U.S. Federal Laws and Regulations

No Federal laws specifically protect the Oregon spotted frog. Section 404 of the Clean Water Act (33 U.S.C. 1251 et seq.) is the primary Federal law that is relevant to the Oregon spotted frog's aquatic habitat. Through a permit process under section 404, the U.S. Army Corps of Engineers (Corps) regulates the discharge of dredged or fill material into waters of the United States, including navigable waters and wetlands that may contain Oregon spotted frogs. However, many actions highly detrimental to Oregon spotted frogs and their habitats, such as irrigation diversion structure construction and maintenance and other activities associated with ongoing farming operations in existing cropped wetlands, are exempt from Clean Water Act requirements.

In Washington and Oregon, current section 404 regulations provide for the issuance of nationwide permits for at least 15 of the 52 categories of activities identified under the nationwide permit program (USACOE 2012a, pp. 1-46), which, for example, could result in the permanent loss of up to 500 ft (150 m) of streambank and 1 ac (0.4 ha) of wetlands (USACOE 2012a, 2012b, 2012c). Projects authorized under a nationwide permit receive minimal public and agency review, and in many cases, agency notification is not required. Individual permits are subject to a more rigorous review, and may be required for nationwide permit activities with more than minimal impacts. Under both the individual and nationwide permit programs, no activities can be authorized if they are likely to directly or indirectly (1) jeopardize the continued existence of a threatened or endangered species, or a species proposed for designation, or (2) destroy or adversely modify the critical habitat of such species, unless section 7 consultation addressing the effects of the proposed activity has been completed. During section 7 consultation, effects to the species itself and aquatic habitat/wetlands would be considered.

For nationwide permits, Corps notification may not be required depending upon the project type and the amount of wetland to be impacted. Impacts to wetlands may be authorized with no compensatory mitigation in some cases. In other cases, wetland impacts may be authorized if the permittee demonstrates the project footprint has been designed to avoid most wetland impacts and unavoidable impacts can be adequately mitigated through wetland creation, restoration, or enhancement. For example, nationwide permits authorize the discharge of fill material into 0.25 ac (0.1 ha) of wetlands with no requirement for compensatory mitigation. In situations where compensatory wetland mitigation is required, in kind mitigation is preferred but not required.

A Washington State wetland mitigation evaluation study (Johnson et al. 2002b, entire) found a resulting net loss of wetlands with or without compensatory mitigation, because wetland creation and enhancement projects were minimally successful or not successful in implementation, nor did they achieve their ecologically relevant measures. In general, most riparian habitat restoration in Washington is targeted toward salmon species and does not include floodplain depression wetlands. In Washington, mitigation sites within the South Fork Nooksack, Samish, and Black River sub-basins have been designed to improve water quality by planting trees and shrubs. Some of these activities have been conducted in Oregon spotted frog breeding habitat. Therefore, an activity that fills Oregon spotted frog habitat could be mitigated by restoring and or creating riparian habitat suitable for fish, but which is not suitable for frogs.

State Laws and Regulations

Washington— Although there is no State Endangered Species Act in Washington, the Washington Fish and Wildlife Commission has the authority to list species (RCW 77.12.020). State-listed species are protected from direct take, but their habitat is not protected (RCW 77.15.120). The Oregon spotted frog was listed as a State endangered species in Washington in August 1997 (Watson et al. 1998, p. 1; 2003, p. 292; WAC 232-12-014). State listings generally consider only the status of the species within the State's borders, and do not depend upon the same considerations as a potential Federal listing. Unoccupied or unsurveyed habitat is not protected unless by County ordinances or other similar rules or laws.

Oregon spotted frogs are a Priority Species under WDFW's Priority Habitats and Species Program (WDFW 2008, pp. 68). As a Priority Species, the Oregon spotted frog may receive some protection of its habitat under environmental reviews of applications for county or municipal development permits and through implementation of priority habitats and species management recommendations. Priority habitat and species management recommendations for this species include maintaining stable water levels and natural flow rates; maintaining vegetation along stream banks or pond edges; avoidance of introducing nonnative amphibians, reptiles, or fish; avoidance of removing algae from rearing areas; avoiding alteration of muddy substrates; controlling stormwater runoff away from frog habitat; avoiding application of pesticides in or adjacent to waterbodies used by Oregon spotted frogs; and surveying within the historical range of the species (Nordstrom and Milner 1997, pp. 6-5—6-6).

The Clean Water Act requires States to set water quality standards to protect beneficial uses, identify sources of pollution in waters that fail to meet State water quality standards (Section 303(d)), and to develop water quality plans to address those pollutants. Although the Clean Water

Act is a Federal law, authority for implementing this law has been delegated to the State. Washington State adopted revised water quality standards for temperature and intergravel dissolved oxygen in December 2006, and the Environmental Protection Agency (EPA) approved these revised standards in February 2008 (EPA 2008). Although candidate species were not the focus, proponents believed that the proposed standards would likely protect native aquatic species. The temperature standards are intended to restore thermal regimes to protect sensitive native salmonids, and, if temperature is not a limiting factor in sustaining viable salmonid populations, other native species would likely be protected (EPA 2007, p. 14).

The State has developed water quality plans for the Lower Nooksack, Samish, and Upper Chehalis Rivers; however, as of 2008 (most recent freshwater listing), portions of the Sumas River; Black Slough in the South Fork Nooksack River sub-basin; portions of the Samish River; segments of the Black River; segments of Dempsey, Allen, and Beaver Creeks in the Black River drainage; and a segment in the upper portion of Trout Lake Creek were listed by the Washington Department of Ecology (WDOE) as not meeting water quality standards for a variety of parameters, including temperature, fecal coliform, pH, and dissolved oxygen (see Factor E discussion). In addition, for the streams/rivers where the temperature or fecal coliform standard is exceeded, the water quality plans call for planting trees and shrubs and excluding cattle, which would not be conducive to the creation and maintenance of emergent vegetation stage conditions necessary for Oregon spotted frog egg-laying habitat (see Factor A discussion).

Oregon— Oregon has a State Endangered Species Act, but the Oregon spotted frog is not State listed. Although this species is on the Oregon sensitive species list and is considered critically sensitive, this designation provides little protection (ODFW 1996, OAR 635-100-0040). A Federal listing does not guarantee a listing under the Oregon State Endangered Species Act; rather a State listing requires a separate rulemaking process and findings made by the Oregon Fish and Wildlife Commission (OAR 635-100-0105 and 635-100-0110).

Although the Clean Water Act is a Federal law, authority for implementing this law has been delegated to the State. Oregon adopted revised water quality standards for temperature, intergravel dissolved oxygen, and anti-degradation in December 2003, and EPA approved these revised standards in March 2004 (EPA 2004). Although candidate species were not the focus, it was believed that the proposed standards would likely protect native aquatic species. The proposed temperature standards are intended to restore thermal regimes to protect sensitive native salmonids and, if temperature is not a limiting factor in sustaining viable salmonid populations, other native species would likely be protected (EPA 2004). In December 2012, EPA approved additions to Oregon's 303(d) list, which includes waterbodies that do not meet water quality standards for multiple parameters (ODEQ 2012). Many of the streams associated with Oregon spotted frog habitat are 303(d) listed by the Oregon Department of Environmental Quality (see Factor E).

Oregon's Removal-Fill Law (ORS 196.795-990) requires people who plan to remove or fill material in waters of the State to obtain a permit from the Department of State Lands. Wetlands and waterways in Oregon are protected by both State and Federal laws. Projects impacting waters often require both a State removal-fill permit, issued by the Department of State Lands (DSL), and a Federal permit issued by the Corps. A permit is required only if 50 cubic yards (cy) or more of fill or removal will occur. The removal fill law does not regulate the draining of wetlands (see "Local Laws and Regulations," below).

Local Laws and Regulations

Washington— The Washington Shoreline Management Act's purpose is "to prevent the inherent harm in an uncoordinated and piecemeal development of the State's shorelines." Shorelines are defined as: All marine waters; streams and rivers with greater than 20 cfs (0.6 cms) mean annual flow; lakes 20 ac or larger; upland areas called shorelands that extend 200 ft (61 m) landward from the edge of these waters; and the following areas when they are associated with one of the previous shorelines: Biological wetlands and river deltas, and some or all of the 100-year floodplain, including all wetlands within the 100-year floodplain. Each city and county with "shorelines of the state" must prepare and adopt a Shoreline Master Program (SMP) that is based on State laws and rules but is tailored to the specific geographic, economic, and environmental needs of the community. The local SMP is essentially a shoreline-specific combined comprehensive plan, zoning ordinance, and development permit system.

The Washington State Growth Management Act of 1990 requires all jurisdictions in the State to designate and protect critical areas. The State defines five broad categories of critical areas, including (a) wetlands; (b) areas with a critical recharging effect on aquifers used for potable water; (c) fish and wildlife habitat conservation areas; (d) frequently flooded areas; and (e) geologically hazardous areas. The County Area Ordinance (CAO) is the county regulation that most directly addresses protection of the critical areas mapped by each county.

Frequently, local government will have adopted zoning regulations and comprehensive land use plans that apply both within and outside shoreline areas. When these codes are applied within the shoreline area, there may be differences in the zoning regulations and the plan policies as compared with the regulations and policies of the SMP. Because the SMP is technically a State law (i.e., WAC), the requirements of the SMP will prevail in the event of a conflict with the local zoning or plan. Generally, however, a conflict will not exist if the zoning or plan requirements are more protective of the shoreline environment than the SMP. For example, if the zoning district allows a density of one unit per acre, and the SMP allows a density of two units per, the requirements of the more restrictive code would prevail.

Within each county in Washington, the SMP and CAO are the regulations that most directly address protection of Oregon spotted frog habitat. A brief discussion of the current SMPs and CAOs for the five counties where Oregon spotted frogs are known to occur follows.

Whatcom County: Whatcom County updated its Shoreline Management Program (known as a Shoreline Master Program in the Growth Management Act) in 2008 (Whatcom County Shoreline Management Program 2008). Based on interpretation of the 2008 Shoreline Management Program, the known Oregon spotted frog occupied locations in the Lower Chilliwack or South Fork Nooksack River sub-basins are not "shorelines." Samish River within Whatcom County is designated as Conservancy Shoreline that provides specific allowed uses and setbacks. Presently, the two primary uses of this area are agricultural and residential, both of which are allowed under the Shoreline Management Program, with some restrictions. Restrictions include shoreline setbacks of 15-20 ft (4.5-6.1 m) and allowance of no more than 10 percent impervious surface (although it is uncertain whether this is applicable on a per-project, per-acre, or per-basin basis). One of the allowed uses is restoration, which is focused on recovery of salmon and bull trout. Many of the restoration actions targeting salmon and bull trout recovery are not conducive to maintaining emergent wetland vegetation stages necessary to maintain Oregon spotted frog egg-laying habitat. Some activities would require a permit that must be reviewed and approved by Whatcom County and the WDOE for consistency.

The Whatcom County CAO that is the most relevant to Oregon spotted frogs applies to wetland areas, which are present in the three sub-basins where Oregon spotted frogs occur in this county. Activities in all wetlands are regulated unless the wetland is 1/10 ac or smaller in size; however, activities that can destroy or modify Oregon spotted frog habitat can still occur under the existing CAO. Activities that are conditionally allowed include surface water discharge; storm water management facilities; storm water conveyance or discharge facilities; public roads, bridges, and trails; single-family developments; and onsite sewage disposal systems. Buffers and mitigation are required, but can be adjusted by the county. In general, wetlands and the associated wetland buffer CAOs target an avoidance strategy, which may not be beneficial to the maintenance of Oregon spotted frog emergent wetland habitat on a long-term basis in areas where reed canarygrass is present. Within the areas occupied by Oregon spotted frogs in the three sub-basins, all breeding habitat is within seasonally flooded areas, which may or may not be defined as wetlands. Rather than an avoidance strategy, these areas may require management actions to remove reed canarygrass in order to maintain breeding habitat and provide for Oregon spotted frog persistence. Within Whatcom County, protective measures for Oregon spotted frogs are afforded under both the SMP and the CAOs, although no measures are specifically directed toward this species.

Skagit County: Skagit County's revisions to its SMP are under review (http://www.skagitcounty.net). Until the revised SMP is approved by WDOE, the 1976 SMP remains in effect (Skagit County SMP 1976). The portion of the Samish River in Skagit County is designated as Rural Shoreline Area, and typified by low overall structural density, and low to moderate intensity of agriculture, residential development, outdoor recreation, and forestry operations uses. This designation is intended to maintain open spaces and opportunities for recreational activities and a variety of uses compatible with agriculture and the shoreline environment. Presently, the two primary uses of the Samish River where Oregon spotted frogs occur are agricultural and residential. With some restrictions, almost all activities are allowed within this designation, and the draining of wetlands is not prohibited. Agricultural users are encouraged to retain vegetation along stream banks. Developments and sand and gravel extractions are allowed provided they are compatible with agricultural uses. These types of activities can be detrimental to Oregon spotted frog breeding habitat.

The Skagit County CAO designates lands adjacent to the Samish River where Oregon spotted frogs are known to occur as Rural Resource or Agricultural. These land designations and the associated allowed activities are intended to provide some protection of hydrological functions, but they are primarily designed to retain a rural setting (low residential density) or to ensure the stability and productivity of agriculture and forestry in the county, which has some benefits to the Oregon spotted frog.

Thurston County: Thurston County's revision of its SMP is currently under way, and until the revised SMP is completed and approved, the 1990 SMP remains in effect (Thurston County SMP 1990). The majority of the areas within the Black River that are known to be occupied by Oregon spotted frogs are either undesignated (primarily the tributaries) or designated as Natural or Conservancy Environments. Two small areas are designated as Urban at the town of Littlerock and along Beaver Creek. Fish Pond Creek, a known Oregon spotted frog breeding location, is within the designated Tumwater Urban Growth Area. Within the Natural Environment designation areas, most activity types are prohibited, although livestock grazing, low-intensity recreation, low-density (1 domicile per 10 ac) residences, and conditional shoreline alterations are allowed. Within Conservancy Environments, most activities are conditionally allowed, and would require a permit that must be reviewed and approved by Thurston County and WDOE for consistency with the SMP.

Thurston County approved a revision to the CAO in July 2012. The Thurston County CAO that is the most relevant to Oregon spotted frogs addresses wetlands, although the Fish and Wildlife Habitat Conservation Areas chapter and the 100-year floodplain and Channel Migration Zone designations are also applicable. Activities in most wetlands are regulated, other than those less than or equal to 1,000 square feet (ft^2) in size (although the county can waive this size threshold if a priority species is known to occur). However, due to State law, the 2012 CAO update did not address agricultural activities, and the jurisdictional wetland size for these activities is 22,000 ft^2

in the rural county, 11,000 ft 2 in Urban Growth Areas, or 2,500 ft 2 if adjacent to a stream or its floodplain. As a result, activities that can destroy or modify Oregon spotted frog habitat may still occur, such as asphalt batch plant construction, new agricultural uses, boat ramps, docks, piers, floats, bridge or culvert projects, clearing-grading-excavation activities, and dredging/removal operations. Buffers and mitigation are required, but can be adjusted by the county. In general, wetlands and the associated wetland buffer CAOs strive toward a no-management approach, which may not be beneficial to the maintenance of Oregon spotted frog emergent wetland habitat on a long-term basis. Within the areas occupied by Oregon spotted frogs in the Black River, all breeding habitat is within seasonally flooded areas, which may or may not be defined as wetlands or high ground water hazard areas (both designations would require set-backs). Rather than an avoidance strategy, these areas may require management actions to remove reed canarygrass in order to maintain egg-laying habitat. Seasonally flooded areas where agricultural uses are existing and ongoing are exempt from review under the CAO; however, expansion of activities may trigger additional review. Within Thurston County, protective measures for Oregon spotted frogs are afforded under both the SMP and CAOs, although no measures are specifically directed toward this species.

Skamania County: Skamania County's revision to its SMP is under way, and until revised, the 1980 SMP is in effect (Skamania County SMP 1980). According to the 1980 SMP, Trout Lake Creek is not a shoreline of Skamania County. The portions of Trout Lake Creek that are in Skamania County have no designated critical areas. Therefore, the SMP and CAO are not applicable to Oregon spotted frog habitat in Skamania County.

Klickitat County: Klickitat County's SMP was adopted in 1998, and revised in 2007 (Klickitat County SMP 2007). Based on the 2007 SMP, only Trout Lake Creek is considered a "shoreline," and within the area occupied by Oregon spotted frogs, regulations for both Natural and Conservancy Environments apply. Within the Natural Environments, most activity types are prohibited, except for nonintensive pasturing or grazing, recreation (access trails/passive uses), bulkheads (conditional uses), and shoreline alterations (conditional). Within Conservancy Environments, most activities are conditionally allowed, and require a permit that must be reviewed and approved by Klickitat County and WDOE for consistency.

Klickitat County's CAO was adopted in 2001, and amended in 2004. Mapping of critical areas was not available, so our analysis includes only wetlands provisions. Activities in all wetlands greater than 2,500 ft 2 (232 m 2) in size are regulated; however, some activities are exempted, including agricultural uses and maintenance of surface water systems (for example, irrigation and drainage ditches). These types of activities can destroy or modify Oregon spotted frog habitat. Buffers and mitigation are required, but can be adjusted by the county. In general, wetlands and the associated wetland buffer CAOs strive toward a no-management approach, which may result in the loss of Oregon spotted frog emergent wetland habitat on a long-term basis. Within the areas occupied by Oregon spotted frogs in Klickitat County, all breeding habitat is within seasonally flooded areas, which may or may not be defined as wetlands. Rather than an avoidance strategy, these areas may require management actions to remove reed canarygrass in order to maintain egg-laying habitat. Within Klickitat County, protective measures for Oregon spotted frogs are afforded under both the SMP and CAOs, although no measures are specifically directed toward this species.

Oregon— In Oregon, the Land Conservation and Development Commission in 1974 adopted Goal 5 as a broad, Statewide planning goal that covers more than a dozen resources, including wildlife habitats and natural areas. Goal 5 and related Oregon Administrative Rules (Chapter 660, Divisions 16 and 23) describe how cities and counties are to plan and zone land to conserve resources listed in the goal. Goal 5 is a required planning process that allows local governments to make decisions about land use regulations and whether to protect the individual resources based upon potential conflicts involving economic, social, environmental, and energy consequences. It does not require minimum levels of protections for natural resources, but does require weighing the various impacts to resources from land use.

Counties in Oregon within the range of Oregon spotted frog may have zoning ordinances that reflect protections set forth during the Goal 5 planning process. The following will briefly discuss these within each county where Oregon spotted frogs are currently known to occur.

Deschutes County: In accordance with the Statewide planning process discussed above, Deschutes County completed a comprehensive plan in 1979, which was updated in 2011, although Oregon spotted frog habitat is not included within the comprehensive plan as a Goal 5 resource site. The comprehensive plan is implemented primarily through zoning. Deschutes County zoning ordinances that regulate the removal and fill of wetlands (18.128.270), development within the floodplain (18.96.100), and siting of structures within 100 ft (30 m) of streams may provide indirect protections to Oregon spotted frog habitat on private lands along the Upper and Little Deschutes Rivers. The Deschutes County zoning regulations do not regulate the draining of wetlands or hydrologic modifications, and the Oregon Division of State Lands (DSL) regulates only actions that involve more than 50 cy (38 m 3) of wetland removal. Therefore, development associated with small wetland removals is neither regulated under the Deschutes County comprehensive plan nor Oregon DSL, which could negatively impact Oregon spotted frog habitat.

Klamath County: Article 57 of the Klamath County Comprehensive Plan Policy (KCCPP) and associated Klamath County Development Code (KCDC) mandates provisions to preserve significant natural and cultural resources; address the economic, social, environmental, and energy consequences of conflicting uses upon significant natural and cultural resources; and permit development in a manner that does not adversely impact identified resource values (KCDC 2005, p. 197). This plan identifies significant wetlands, riparian areas, Class I streams, and fish habitat as a significant resource and identifies potentially conflicting uses including shoreline development or alteration, removal of riparian vegetation, filling or removing material, in-stream modification, introduction of pollutants, water impoundments, and drainage or channelization (KCCPP 2005, pp. 33-34, KCDC 2005, p. 199). All land uses that represent these conflicting uses are reviewed and applicants must clearly demonstrate that the proposed use will not negatively impact the resource (KCDC 2005, p. 200; KCCPP 2005, p. 25). However, all accepted farm practices or forest practices are exempt from this provision (KCDC 2005, p. 198), including (but not limited to) buildings, wineries, mineral exploration, and, under certain circumstances, the establishment of golf courses and agricultural and commercial industries (KCDC 2005, pp. 160-163, 176-177). If any of these practices disturb less than 50 cy (38.2 m 3) of wetlands, they are not regulated by either KCCPP or Oregon DSL. Therefore, the development associated with small wetland removals could negatively impact Oregon spotted frog habitat.

Jackson County: No specific county regulations pertain to wetlands within Jackson County ordinances. This county relies on the Oregon DSL to regulate the development and protection of wetlands (Skyles 2012, pers. comm.).

Summary of Existing Regulatory Mechanisms

The existing regulatory mechanisms described above are not sufficient to reduce or remove threats to the Oregon spotted frog habitat, particularly habitat loss and degradation. The lack of essential habitat protection under Federal, State, Provincial, and local laws leaves this species at continued risk of habitat loss and degradation in British Columbia, Washington, and Oregon. The review of impacts to wetlands under the Clean Water Act is minimal, and several occupied sub-basins in Washington and Oregon do not meet water quality standards. In many cases, laws and regulations that pertain to retention and restoration of wetland and riverine areas are designed to be beneficial to fish species, specifically salmonids, resulting in the unintentional elimination or degradation of Oregon spotted frog habitat. For example, CAOs in some Washington counties prohibit grazing within the riparian corridor, which is an active management technique that, properly applied, can be used to control invasive reed canarygrass.

Additional regulatory flexibility would be desirable for actively maintaining habitat in those areas essential for the conservation of Oregon spotted frog. We note that the area where these potential incompatibilities apply are limited in scope (i.e., approximately 5,000 ac (2,000 ha) and 20 mi (33 km) along the Black Slough and Sumas, Samish, and Black Rivers in Washington), because the area inhabited by Oregon spotted frogs is quite small relative to the extensive range of salmonids. In other cases, no regulations address threats related to the draining or development of wetlands or hydrologic modifications, which can eliminate or degrade Oregon spotted frog habitat. In summary, degradation of habitat for the Oregon spotted frog is ongoing despite existing regulatory mechanisms. These regulatory mechanisms have been insufficient to significantly reduce or remove the threats to the Oregon spotted frog. Therefore, based upon our review of the best information available, we conclude that the existing regulatory mechanisms are inadequate to reduce the threats to the Oregon spotted frog.

Factor E. Other Natural or Manmade Factors Affecting Its Continued Existence

Site Size and Isolation/Population Turnover Rates/Breeding Effort Concentrations and Site Fidelity

Most species' populations fluctuate naturally in response to weather events, disease, predation, or other factors. These factors, however, have less impact on a species with a wide and continuous distribution. In addition, smaller, isolated populations are generally more likely to be extirpated by stochastic events and genetic drift (Lande 1988, pp. 1456-1458). Many of the Oregon spotted frog breeding locations comprise fewer than 50 adult frogs, are isolated from other breeding locations, and may already be stressed by other factors, such as drought or predation, and are then more vulnerable to random, naturally occurring events. Where Oregon spotted frog locations have small population sizes and are isolated, their vulnerability to extirpation from factors such as fluctuating water levels, disease, and predation increases.

Funk et al. (2008, p. 205) found low genetic variation in Oregon spotted frogs, which likely reflects small effective population sizes, historical or current genetic bottlenecks, and/or low gene flow among populations. Genetic work by Blouin et al. (2010) indicates low genetic diversity within and high genetic differentiation among each of the six Oregon spotted frog groups (British Columbia, Chehalis and Columbia drainages, Camas Prairie, central Oregon Cascades, and the Klamath Basin). This pattern of genetic fragmentation is likely caused by low connectivity between sites and naturally small populations sizes. Gene flow is very limited between locations, especially if separated by 6 mi (10 km) or more, and at the larger scale, genetic groups have the signature of complete isolation (Blouin et al. 2010, p. 2187). At least two of the locations sampled by Blouin et al. (2010) (Camas Prairie and Trout Lake) show indications of recent genetic drift.

Modeling across a variety of amphibian taxa suggests that pond-breeding frogs have high temporal variances of population abundances and high local extinction rates relative to other groups of amphibians, with smaller frog populations undergoing disproportionately large fluctuations in abundance (Green 2003, pp. 339-341). The vulnerability of Oregon spotted frog egg masses to fluctuating water levels (Hayes et al. 2000, pp. 10-12; Pearl and Bury 2000, p. 10), the vulnerability of post-metamorphic stages to predation (Hayes 1994, p. 25), and low overwintering survival (Hallock and Pearson 2001, p. 8) can contribute to relatively rapid population turnovers, suggesting Oregon spotted frogs are particularly vulnerable to local extirpations from stochastic events and chronic sources of mortality (Pearl and Hayes 2004, p. 11). The term "rapid population turnovers" refers to disproportionately large fluctuations in abundance.

Oregon spotted frogs concentrate their breeding efforts in relatively few locations (Hayes et al. 2000, pp. 5-6; McAllister and White 2001, p. 11). For example, Hayes et al. (2000, pp. 5-6) found that 2 percent of breeding sites accounted for 19 percent of the egg masses at the Conboy Lake NWR. Similar breeding concentrations have been found elsewhere in Washington and in Oregon. Moreover, Oregon spotted frogs exhibit relatively high fidelity to breeding locations, using the same seasonal pools every year and often using the same egg-laying sites. In years of extremely high or low water, the frogs may use alternative sites. For example, the Trout Lake Creek and Conboy Lake frogs return to traditional breeding areas every year, but the egg-laying sites change based on water depth at the time of breeding. A stochastic event that impacts any one of these breeding locations could significantly reduce the Oregon spotted frog population associated with that sub-basin.

Egg mass count data suggest a positive correlation and significant link between site size and Oregon spotted frog breeding population size (Pearl and Hayes 2004, p. 12). Larger sites are more likely to provide the seasonal microhabitats required by Oregon spotted frogs, have a more reliable prey base, and include overwintering habitat. The minimum amount of habitat thought to be required to maintain an Oregon spotted frog population is about 10 ac (4 ha) (Hayes 1994, Part II pp. 5 and 7). Smaller sites generally have a small number of frogs and, as described above, are more vulnerable to extirpation. Some sites in Oregon are at or below the 10-ac (4-ha) threshold; however, Pearl and Hayes (2004, p. 14) believe that these sites were historically subpopulations within a larger breeding complex and Oregon spotted frogs may only be persisting in these small sites because the sites exchange migrants or seasonal habitat needs are provided nearby.

Movement studies suggest Oregon spotted frogs are limited in their overland dispersal and potential to recolonize sites. Oregon spotted frog movements are associated with aquatic connections (Watson et al. 2003, p. 295; Pearl and Hayes 2004, p. 15). However, within 10 of the 15 occupied sub-basins, one or more of the known breeding locations are isolated and separated by at least 3.1 mi (5 km) (see Life History, above), and within 9 of the 15 sub-basins, one or more of the known breeding locations are isolated and separated by at least 6 mi (10 km), the distance over which gene flow is extremely low (see Taxonomy, above). In many instances the intervening habitat lacks the substantial hydrological connections that would allow Oregon spotted frog movement. In addition, widespread predaceous fish introductions within these corridors pose a very high risk to frogs that do try to move between known locations. Therefore, should a stochastic event occur that results in the extirpation of an area, natural recolonization is unlikely unless another known location is hydrologically connected and within 3.1 mi (5 km).

In British Columbia, the distance between the Morris Valley, Mountain Slough, and Maria Slough locations is about 8 km and each of these locations is 50-60 km from Maintenance Detachment Aldergrove, making all of the known populations isolated from one another (COSFRT 2012, p. 15). In addition, suitable wetland habitat between any two of these locations is highly fragmented, and movement between populations is unlikely to occur. Based on this information and the small number of breeding individuals (fewer than 350), the Canadian Oregon spotted frog recovery team found that the risk from demographic and environmental stochastic events is high and could result in further local extirpations (COSFRT 2012, p. v).

In five of the six extant sub-basins in Washington, Oregon spotted frogs are restricted to one watershed within the sub-basin. Within four of these sub-basins (South Fork Nooksack, Samish, White Salmon, and Middle Klickitat Rivers), the known breeding locations are aquatically connected, such that movements could occur and facilitate genetic exchange. In the Lower Chilliwack, Oregon spotted frogs are currently known to occur from only one breeding location in one watershed (Sumas River). There may be additional locations within 3.1 mi (5 km) that are aquatically connected, but further surveys would be needed in order to make this determination. In the Black River, known breeding locations occur along the mainstem, as well as in six tributaries. Oregon spotted frogs in Fish Pond Creek are likely isolated from Oregon spotted frogs in the rest of the Black River system due to changes in the outflow of Black Lake. Black Lake Ditch was constructed in 1922, and a pipeline at the outlet of the Black Lake to Black River was constructed in the 1960s; both of these structures changed the flow such that Black Lake drains to the north, except during high flows rather than down the Black River as it did historically (Foster Wheeler Environmental Corporation 2003, pp. 2, 3, 5, 24). Oregon spotted frogs in the other five tributaries may also be isolated from each other because there is little evidence that the frogs use the Black River to move between tributaries, although breeding locations in these tributaries are aquatically connected via the Black River.

In Oregon, two of the eight extant sub-basins contain single, isolated populations of Oregon spotted frogs: Lower Deschutes River (i.e., Camas Prairie) and Middle Fork Willamette River (i.e., Gold Lake). The McKenzie River sub-basin contains two populations of Oregon spotted frogs that are in close proximity but have no apparent hydrologic connection to each other or to populations in other sub-basins. In the Deschutes River Basin, Oregon spotted frog breeding sites are found throughout two sub-basins: The Upper Deschutes River and the Little Deschutes River. These two sub-basins are aquatically connected at the confluence of the Little Deschutes River and the mainstem Deschutes River below Wickiup Reservoir. Genetic exchange likely occurs between Oregon spotted frogs on the lower reach of the Little Deschutes River and those along the Deschutes River at Sunriver where breeding occurs within 3.1 mi (5 km). The Wickiup dam and regulated flows out of the reservoir limit connectivity for Oregon spotted frogs to move within the Upper Deschutes River sub-basin, such that connectivity between the populations above and below the dam are unlikely. There are at least five breeding locations below Wickiup Reservoir, two of which are within 6 mi (10 km) but separated by a waterfall along the Deschutes River. Above Wickiup Reservoir, there are approximately six clusters of breeding sites that may be isolated from each other by lack of hydrologic connectivity (i.e., lakes without outlets) or distances greater than 6 mi (10 km).

In the Little Deschutes River sub-basin, approximately 23 known breeding locations are within five watersheds: Upper, Middle and Lower Little Deschutes River; Crescent Creek; and Long Prairie. Most breeding locations throughout the Little Deschutes River sub-basin are within 6 mi (10 km) of each other, and, given that much of the private land is unsurveyed, the distance between breeding areas is likely smaller. In the lower reach of the Little Deschutes River near the confluence with the Deschutes River where more extensive surveys have been conducted, breeding sites are within 3.1 mi (5 km). Wetland complexes are extensive and continuous along the Little Deschutes River and its tributaries, which likely provides connectivity between breeding areas. Regulated flows out of Crescent Lake may affect the aquatic connectivity between breeding locations, although the impacts to Oregon spotted frog connectivity are not fully understood. The Long Prairie watershed also has been hydrologically altered by the historical draining of wetlands and ditching to supply irrigation water. Connectivity between three known breeding locations within this watershed is likely affected by the timing and duration of regulated flows, and historic ditching for irrigation.

Oregon spotted frogs are found in six watersheds within three sub-basins of the Klamath River Basin in Oregon (Williamson River, Upper Klamath Lake, and Upper Klamath). Within the Williamson River sub-basin, individuals in the Jack Creek watershed are isolated from other populations due to lack of hydrologic connectivity. The Klamath Marsh and Upper Williamson populations are aquatically connected such that movements could occur and facilitate genetic exchange, although this presumed gene flow has not been demonstrated by recent genetic work (Robertson and Funk 2012, p. 10).

The Upper Klamath Lake sub-basin populations are found in two watersheds: Wood River and Klamath Lake. Populations within and adjacent to the Wood River are aquatically connected and genetically similar (Robertson and Funk 2012, p. 10). However, while the Wood River populations and the Klamath Lake populations have genetic similarities (Robertson and Funk 2012, pp. 10, 11), altered hydrologic connections, distances (>6 mi (terrestrial) (10 km)), and invasive species have created inhospitable habitat. These conditions make it unlikely that individual frogs are able to move between watersheds or establish additional breeding complexes along the current hydrologic system. The only potential for hydrologic connectivity and movement between populations in the Klamath Lake populations is between Sevenmile Creek and Crane Creek, and between the individual breeding complexes on the Wood River in the Wood River watershed. The Upper Klamath sub-basin's Parsnip Lakes and Buck Lake populations are isolated from each other and the other Klamath Basin populations (Robertson and Funk 2012, p. 5) due to great hydrological distances (>20 mi (32 km)) and barriers (inhospitable habitat and dams).

Site size and isolation/population turnover rates/breeding effort concentrations and site fidelity conclusion—Historically, Oregon spotted frogs were likely distributed throughout a watershed, occurred in multiple watersheds within a sub-basin, and adjusted their breeding areas as natural disturbances, such as flood events and beaver activity, shifted the location and amount of appropriate habitat. Currently, Oregon spotted frogs are restricted in their range within most occupied sub-basins (in some cases only occurring in one watershed), and breeding areas are isolated (greater than dispersal distance apart). Many of the Oregon spotted frog breeding locations across the range comprise fewer than 50 adult frogs and are isolated from other breeding locations. Genetic work indicates low genetic diversity within and high genetic differentiation among the six Oregon spotted frog groups. Each of these groups have the signature of complete isolation, and two show indications of recent genetic drift (a change in the gene pool of a small population that takes place strictly by chance). Oregon spotted frogs can experience rapid population turnovers because of their breeding location fidelity and vulnerability to fluctuating water levels, predation, and low overwinter survival. A stochastic event at any one of these small, isolated breeding locations could significantly reduce the Oregon spotted frog population associated with that sub-basin. Therefore, based on the best information available, we consider small site size and isolation and small population sizes to be a threat to the Oregon spotted frog.

Water Quality and Contamination

Poor water quality and water contamination are playing a role in the decline of Oregon spotted frogs, and water quality concerns have been specifically noted within six of the occupied sub-basins (see Table 2 under Cumulative Effects from Factors A through E, below, and Factor D discussion, above), although data specific to this species are limited. Because of this limitation, we have examined responses by similar amphibians as a surrogate for impacts on Oregon spotted frogs. Studies comparing responses of amphibians to other aquatic species have demonstrated that amphibians are as sensitive as, and often more sensitive than, other species when exposed to aquatic contaminants (Boyer and Grue 1995, p. 353). Immature amphibians absorb contaminants during respiration through the skin and gills. They may also ingest contaminated prey. Pesticides, heavy metals, nitrates and nitrites, and other contaminants introduced into the aquatic environment from urban and agricultural areas are known to negatively affect various life stages of a wide range of amphibian species, including ranid frogs (Hayes and Jennings 1986, p. 497; Boyer and

Grue 1995, pp. 353-354; Hecnar 1995, pp. 2133-2135; Materna et al. 1995, pp. 616-618; NBII 2005; Mann et al. 2009, p. 2904). Exposure to pesticides can lower an individual's immune function, which increases the risk of disease or possible malformation (Stark 2005, p. 21; Mann et al. 2009, pp. 2905, 2909). In addition, it has been demonstrated that some chemicals reduce growth and delay development.

A reduction of growth or development would prolong an individual's larval period, thus making it more susceptible to predators for a longer period of time or resulting in immobility during periods of time when movement between habitats may be necessary (Mann et al. 2009, p. 2906). Many of the described effects from pesticides are sublethal but ultimately may result in the mortality of the exposed individuals as described above. Furthermore, the results of several studies have suggested that, while the impacts of individual chemicals on amphibians are sublethal, a combination or cocktail of a variety of chemicals may be lethal (Mann et al. 2009, p. 2913; Bishop et al. 2010, p. 1602). The use of pesticides may be occurring throughout the range of the Oregon spotted frog due to the species' overlap with agricultural and urban environments; however, information regarding the extent, methods of application, and amounts applied is not available. Therefore, we are unable to make an affirmative determination at this time that pesticides are a threat.

There are two agents commonly used for mosquito abatement within the range of Oregon spotted frog: Bacillus var. israelensis (Bti) and methoprene. Bti is a bacterial agent that has no record of adverse direct effects on amphibians, but methoprene has been historically linked to abnormalities in southern leopard frogs (Lithobates utricularia), including completely or partially missing hind limbs, discoloration, and missing eyes. Missing eyes and delayed development in northern cricket frogs (Acris crepitans) have also been linked to methoprene (Stark 2005, p. 20). However, a recent scientific literature review suggests that methoprene is not ultimately responsible for frog malformations (Mann et al. 2009, pp. 2906-2907). The findings of this review suggest that, in order for malformations to occur, the concentration of methoprene in the water would induce mortality (Mann et al. 2009, p. 2906).

We also evaluated the indirect effect that Bti and methoprene may have on Oregon spotted frogs by reducing their insect prey species. When used for mosquito abatement, both Bti and methoprene most strongly affect flies belonging to the suborder Nematocera (the thread-horned flies), which includes mosquitos, but may also other chironomid flies such as non-biting midges (Chironomidae) (Hershey et al. 1998, p. 42; Lawler et al. 2000, p. 177; Rochlin et al. 2011, pp. 11-13). We compiled information on the number of insect orders recorded as present during stomach content studies (Licht 1986a, p. 28; Pearl and Hayes 2002, pp. 145-147; Pearl et al. 2005a, p. 37) and then examined the proportion of the order (diptera; flies) primarily affected by Bti and methoprene in relation to the rest of the recorded diet of the Oregon spotted frog. While there are not many data to consider, the kinds of flies most commonly affected compose a small portion of the overall diet of the Oregon spotted frogs that were included in the stomach content studies. We conclude that Bti and methoprene, applied as recommended for mosquito control, are likely to have a negligible effect on Oregon spotted frogs due to the diversity of the species' diet. This is our conclusion for this species only. We do not assume that these agents could not present a threat to other species of frogs that are more dependent on the nematoceran diptera that Bti and methoprene do negatively affect. Therefore, based on the best available information, we do not consider Bti or methoprene to be a threat to Oregon spotted frogs.

Although the effects on amphibians of rotenone, which is used to remove undesirable fish from lakes, are poorly understood, mortality likely occurs at treatment levels used on fish (McAllister et al. 1999, p. 21). The role of rotenone treatments in the disappearance of Oregon spotted frogs from historical sites is unknown; however, some studies indicate that amphibians might be less sensitive than fish and might be capable of recovering from exposure to rotenone (Mullin et al. 2004, pp. 305-306; Walston and Mullin 2007, p. 65). However, these studies did not measure the effects on highly aquatic amphibians, like the Oregon spotted frog. In fall of 2011, the ODFW used rotenone to remove goldfish from a small pond adjacent to Crane Prairie Reservoir. In April 2012, approximately 40 spotted frog egg masses were located in the pond, where there had been no prior record of Oregon spotted frog occupancy in the past (Wray 2012, pers. comm.). No rotenone treatments in Cascade lakes occupied by Oregon spotted frog are planned in the near future (Hodgson 2012, pers. comm.), and to date, in the Upper Klamath Lake sub-basin, no fish killing agents have been applied within Oregon spotted frog habitat (Banish 2012, pers. comm.). Therefore, based on the best available information, we do not consider rotenone to be a threat to Oregon spotted frogs.

Water acidity (low pH) can inhibit fertilization and embryonic development in amphibians, reduce their growth and survival through physiological alterations, and produce developmental anomalies (Hayes and Jennings 1986, pp. 498-499; Boyer and Grue 1995, p. 353). A low pH may enhance the effects of other factors, such as activating heavy metals in sediments. An elevated pH, acting singly or in combination with other factors such as low dissolved oxygen, high water temperatures, and elevated un-ionized ammonia levels, may have detrimental effects on developing frog embryos (Boyer and Grue 1995, p. 354). Concerns about pH levels have been identified in sub-basins occupied by the Oregon spotted frog.

Required dissolved oxygen levels for Oregon spotted frogs have not been evaluated; however, a number of studies have been conducted on amphibians that indicate that the amount of dissolved oxygen can affect all life stages. Low oxygen levels can affect the rate of egg development, time to hatching, and development stage at hatching. For example, Mills and Barnhart (1999, p. 182) found that embryos of two salamanders developed more slowly and hatching was delayed. In contrast, in two ranid frog species, low oxygen levels resulted in embryos hatching sooner and in a less developed stage (Mills and Barnhart 1999, p. 182). As dissolved oxygen levels decreased below 4.0 to 4.25 parts per million, Wassersug and Seibert (1975, pp. 90-93), found tadpoles of Rana pipiens and Bufo woodhousii swam to the surface (not a normal behavior), and all remained at the surface at levels below 2.0 parts per million. Similarly, Moore and Townsend (1998, p. 332) found that decreasing oxygen levels increased the number of times Rana clamitans tadpoles surfaced and the amount of time spent at the surface. This behavior increased the risk of predation because signficantly more Rana clamitans tadpoles were eaten when mean oxygen levels were at or below 2.7 mg/L (Moore and Townsend 1998, p. 332). Ranid species have been found to use overwintering microhabitat with well-oxygenated waters (Ultsch et al. 2000, p. 315; Lamoureux and Madison 1999, p. 434), although some evidence indicates that Oregon spotted frogs can tolerate levels at or somewhat below 2.0 mg/L during the winter for short periods (Hayes et al. 2001, pp. 20-22; Risenhoover et al. 2001b, pp. 17-18).

Marco et al. (1999, p. 2838) demonstrated the strong sensitivity of Oregon spotted frog tadpoles to nitrate and nitrite ions in laboratory experiments, and suggested that nitrogen-based chemical fertilizers may have contributed to the species' decline in the lowland areas of its distribution. This research suggests that the recommended maximum levels of nitrates (10 milligrams/Liter (mg/L)) and nitrites (1 mg/L) in drinking water are moderately to highly toxic for Oregon spotted frogs, indicating that EPA water quality standards do not protect sensitive amphibian species (Marco et al. 1999, p. 2838). In the Marco et al. study, Oregon spotted frog tadpoles did not show a rapid adverse effect to nitrate ions, but at day 15 of exposure they reflected high sensitivity followed by synchronous death. Many public water supplies in the United States contain levels of nitrate that routinely exceed concentrations of 10 mg/L of nitrate; the median lethal concentrations for aquatic larvae of the Oregon spotted frog is less than 10 mg/L (Marco et al. 1999, p. 2838). Grazing is one source of nitrates and nitrites; according to the EPA, the major sources of nitrates in drinking water are runoff from fertilizer use, leaking from septic tanks and sewage, and erosion of natural deposits. Most currently known occupied sites for Oregon spotted frog are located in areas where residential septic tanks are used and farming practices include fertilizer application and grazing.

Elevated sources of nutrient inputs into river and wetland systems can result in eutrophic (nutrient-rich) conditions, characterized by increased productivity, such as blooms of algae, that can produce a high pH and low dissolved oxygen. Increased eutrophic conditions in the Upper Klamath Lake sub-basin may have contributed to the absence of Oregon spotted frogs. Beginning in 2002, algal blooms, poor water quality, and low dissolved oxygen were documented in Jack Creek, during which a decline in Oregon spotted frog reproduction was also documented (Oertley 2005, pers. comm.).

Water quality concerns have been documented in several waterbodies occupied by the Oregon spotted frog. In Washington, portions of the Sumas River; Black Slough in the South Fork Nooksack sub-basin; portions of the Samish River; segments of the Black River; segments of Dempsey, Allen, and Beaver Creeks in the Black River sub-basin; and a segment in the upper portion of Trout Lake Creek are listed by the WDOE as not meeting water quality standards for a variety of parameters, including temperature, fecal coliform, pH, and dissolved oxygen. In Oregon, many of the streams associated with Oregon spotted frog habitat are listed by the Oregon Department of Environmental Quality as not meeting water quality standards for multiple parameters: (1) Little Deschutes River—temperature, dissolved oxygen, chlorophyll A, pH, aquatic weeds or algae; (2) Deschutes River—temperature, dissolved oxygen, turbidity, sedimentation; (3) Middle Fork Willamette River—sedimentation; (4) Upper Klamath—temperature; and (5) Williamson River—sedimentation.

In British Columbia, Oregon spotted frogs at Morris Valley, Mountain Slough, and Maria Slough are in largely agricultural areas. Agricultural runoff includes fertilizers (including manure); runoff or percolation into the groundwater from manure piles (Rouse et al. 1999); and spraying of agricultural chemicals such as pesticides or insecticides (including Bacillus thuringiensis bacterium) or fungicides (used by blueberry producers), including wind-borne chemicals. Water-borne sewage and non-point source runoff from housing and urban areas that include nutrients, toxic chemicals, and/or sediments may also be increasing in intensity. Additional sources of contaminants may include chemical spraying during forestry activities, maintenance of power line corridors, or disruption of normal movements of nutrients by forestry activities (Canadian Recovery Strategy (COSFRT) 2012, p. 21). The COSFRT (2012, p. 17) identifies pollution associated with agricultural and forestry effluents as being (1) high impact; (2) large in scope; (3) serious in severity; (4) high in timing; and (5) a stress that has direct and indirect mortality results. One of the recovery objectives is to coordinate with the Minister of Agriculture to implement supporting farming practices and environmental farm plans options to decrease agrochemical and nutrient pollution into Oregon spotted frog habitat and work with all levels of government, land managers, and private landowners to inform and encourage best practices and ensure compliance in relation to water quality, hydrology, and land use practice (COSFRS 2012, p. 34).

Although more research is needed, Johnson et al. (2002a; Johnson and Chase 2004) state that eutrophication associated with elevated nitrogen (and phosphorus) has been linked with increased snail populations. Johnson and Chase (2004, p. 522) point to elevated levels of nutrients (particularly phosphorus) from agricultural fertilizers and cattle grazing in freshwater ecosystems as causing shifts in the composition of aquatic snails from small species to larger species. These larger species serve as intermediate hosts for a parasite (Ribeiroia ondatrae), which causes malformations in amphibians (see "Disease" under Factor C discussion, above).

Water quality and contamination conclusion—Although pesticides are known to affect various life stages of the Oregon spotted frog, the impact of this potential threat is undetermined at this time. We do not consider rotenone or methoprene to be threats to the species.

Oregon spotted frogs are highly aquatic throughout their life cycle, and are thus likely to experience extended exposure to any waterborne contaminants. Poor water quality parameters and contaminants may act singly or in combination with other factors to result in inhibited fertilization and embryonic development, developmental anomalies, or reduced growth and survival. More work on the species' ecotoxicology is warranted. However, reduced water quality is documented in a number of occupied sub-basins, and where this overlap occurs we consider poor water quality and contaminants to be threats to the Oregon spotted frog.

Hybridization

Hybridization between Oregon spotted frogs and closely related frog species is unlikely to affect the survival of the Oregon spotted frog. Natural hybridization between Oregon spotted frogs and Cascade frogs has been demonstrated experimentally and verified in nature (Haertel and Storm 1970, pp. 436-444; Green 1985, p. 263). However, the offspring are infertile, and the two species seldom occur together. Hybridization between Oregon spotted frogs and red-legged frogs has also been confirmed (I.C. Phillipsen and K. McAllister cited in Hallock 2013, p. 7), but it is unknown if the hybrids are fertile. Because Oregon spotted frog and Columbia spotted frog populations are not known to occur together, based on the best available information, we do not consider hybridization to be a threat to Oregon spotted frogs.

Climate Change

Our analyses under the Act include consideration of ongoing and projected changes in climate. The terms "climate" and "climate change" are defined by the Intergovernmental Panel on Climate Change (IPCC). The term "climate" refers to the mean and variability of different types of weather conditions over time, with 30 years being a typical period for such measurements, although shorter or longer periods also may be used (IPCC 2007a, p. 78). The term "climate change" thus refers to a change in the mean or variability of one or more measures of climate (e.g., temperature or precipitation) that persists for an extended period, typically decades or longer, whether the change is due to natural variability, human activity, or both (IPCC 2007a, p. 78).

Scientific measurements spanning several decades demonstrate that changes in climate are occurring, and that the rate of change has been faster since the 1950s. Examples include warming of the global climate system, and substantial increases in precipitation in some regions of the world and decreases in other regions. (For these and other examples, see IPCC 2007a, p. 30; Solomon et al. 2007, pp. 35-54, 82-85). Results of scientific analyses presented by the IPCC show that most of the observed increase in global average temperature since the mid-20th century cannot be explained by natural variability in climate, and is "very likely" (defined by the IPCC as 90 percent or higher probability) due to the observed increase in greenhouse gas (GHG) concentrations in the atmosphere as a result of human activities, particularly carbon dioxide emissions from use of fossil fuels (IPCC 2007a, pp. 5-6 and figures SPM.3 and SPM.4; Solomon et al. 2007, pp. 21-35). Further confirmation of the role of GHGs comes from analyses by Huber and Knutti (2011, p. 4), who concluded it is extremely likely that approximately 75 percent of global warming since 1950 has been caused by human activities.

Scientists use a variety of climate models, which include consideration of natural processes and variability, as well as various scenarios of potential levels and timing of GHG emissions, to evaluate the causes of changes already observed and to project future changes in temperature and other climate conditions (e.g., Meehl et al. 2007, entire; Ganguly et al. 2009, pp. 11555, 15558; Prinn et al. 2011, pp. 527, 529). All combinations of models and emissions scenarios yield very similar projections of increases in the most common measure of climate change, average global surface temperature (commonly known as global warming), until about 2030. Although projections of the magnitude and rate of warming differ after about 2030, the overall trajectory of all the projections is one of increased global warming through the end of this century, even for the projections based on scenarios that assume that GHG emissions will stabilize or decline. Thus, strong scientific data support projections that warming will continue through the 21st century, and that the magnitude and rate of change will be influenced substantially by the extent of GHG emissions (IPCC 2007a, pp. 44-45; Meehl et al. 2007, pp. 760-764, 797-811; Ganguly et al. 2009, pp. 15555-15558; Prinn et al. 2011, pp. 527, 529). (See IPCC 2007b, p. 8, for a summary of other global projections of climate-related changes, such as frequency of heat waves and changes in precipitation. Also see IPCC 2012 (entire) for a summary of observations and projections of extreme climate events.)

Various changes in climate may have direct or indirect effects on species. These effects may be positive, neutral, or negative, and they may change over time, depending on the species and other relevant considerations, such as interactions of climate with other variables (e.g., habitat fragmentation) (IPCC 2007, pp. 8-14, 18-19). Identifying likely effects often involves aspects of climate change vulnerability analysis. Vulnerability refers to the degree to which a species (or system) is susceptible to, and unable to cope with, adverse effects of climate change, including climate variability and extremes. Vulnerability is a function of the type, magnitude, and rate of climate change and variation to which a species is exposed, its sensitivity, and its adaptive capacity (IPCC 2007a, p. 89; see also Glick et al. 2011, pp. 19-22). No single method for conducting such analyses applies to all situations (Glick et al. 2011, p. 3). We use our expert judgment and appropriate analytical approaches to weigh relevant information, including uncertainty, in our consideration of various aspects of climate change.

As is the case with all stressors that we assess, even if we conclude that a species is currently affected or is likely to be affected in a negative way by one or more climate-related impacts, the species does not necessarily meet the definition of an "endangered species" or a "threatened species" under the Act. If a species is listed as an endangered or threatened species, knowledge regarding the vulnerability of the species to, and known or anticipated impacts from, climate-associated changes in environmental conditions can be used to help devise appropriate strategies for its recovery.

Global climate projections are informative, and, in some cases, the only or the best scientific information available for us to use. However, projected changes in climate and related impacts can vary substantially across and within different regions of the world (e.g., IPCC 2007a, pp. 8-12). Therefore, we use "downscaled" projections when they are available and have been developed through appropriate scientific procedures, because such projections provide higher resolution information that is more relevant to spatial scales used for analyses of a given species (see Glick et al. 2011, pp. 58-61, for a discussion of downscaling). With regard to our analysis for the Oregon spotted frog, downscaled projections are available.

The climate in the PNW has already experienced a warming of 0.8 degrees Celsius (C) (1.4 degrees Fahrenheit (F)) during the 20th century (Mote et al. 2008, p. 3). Using output from eight climate models, the PNW is projected to warm further by 0.6 to 1.9 degrees C (1.1 to 3.4 degrees F) by the 2020s, and 0.9 to 2.9 degrees C (1.6 to 5.2 degrees F) by the 2040s (Mote et al. 2008, pp. 5-6). Additionally, the majority of models project wetter winters and drier summers (Mote et al. 2008, p. 7), and of greatest consequence, a reduction in regional snowpack, which supplies water for ecosystems during the dry summer (Mote et al. 2003). The small summertime precipitation increases projected by a minority of models do not change the fundamentally dry summers of the PNW and do not lessen the increased drying of the soil column brought by higher temperatures (Mote et al. 2003, p. 8).

Watersheds that are rain dominated (such as the Fraser River in British Columbia and the Black River in Washington) will likely experience higher winter streamflow because of increases in average winter precipitation, but overall will experience relatively little change with respect to streamflow timing (Elsner et al. 2010, p. 248). Water temperatures for western Washington are generally cooler than those in the interior Columbia basin; however, climate change predictions indicate the summertime stream temperatures exceeding 19.5 degrees C (67.1 degrees F) will increase, although by a smaller fraction than the increases in the interior Columbia basin (Mantua et al. 2010, p. 199).

Transient basins (mixed rain- and snowmelt-dominant usually in mid elevations, such as Lower Chilliwack, SF Nooksack, White Salmon, and Middle Klickitat Rivers sub-basins in Washington) will likely experience significant shifts in streamflow and water temperature, becoming rain dominant as winter precipitation falls more as rain and less as snow, and undergo more severe summer low-flow periods and more frequent days with intense winter flooding (Elsner et al. 2010, pp. 248, 252, 255; Mantua et al. 2010, entire).

Snowmelt-dominated watersheds, such as White Salmon in Washington and the Upper Deschutes, Little Deschutes, and Klamath River sub-basins in Oregon, will likely become transient, resulting in reduced peak spring streamflow, increased winter streamflow, and reduced late summer flow (Littell et al. 2009, p. 8). In snowmelt-dominated watersheds that prevail in the higher altitude catchments and in much of the interior Columbia Basin, flood risk will likely decrease and summer low flows will decrease in most rivers under most scenarios (Littell et al. 2009, p. 13).

In Washington, the snow water equivalent measured on April 1 is projected to decrease by 28 to 30 percent across the State by the 2020s, 38 to 46 percent by the 2040s, and 56 to 70 percent by the 2080s, and the areas with elevations below 3,280 ft (1,000 m) will experience the largest decreases in snowpack, with reductions of 68 to 80 percent by the 2080s (Elsner et al. 2010, p. 244). In the Puget Trough sub-basins, summertime soil moisture will decrease as a result of the warming climate and reduced snowpack. While annual precipitation is projected to slightly increase across the State, by 3.4 percent by the 2080s, the seasonality of the precipitation will change more dramatically with increased winter and decreased summer precipitation, with most of the precipitation falling between October and March (Elsner et al. 2010, p. 247).

Climate change models predict that water temperatures will rise throughout Oregon as air temperatures increase into the 21st century. A decline in summer stream flow may exacerbate water temperature increases as the lower volume of water absorbs solar radiation (Chang and Jones 2010, p. 134).

Analyses of the hydrologic responses of the upper Deschutes basin (including the Upper and Little Deschutes River sub-basins) and the Klamath Basin to climate change scenarios indicates that the form of precipitation will shift from predominately snow to rain and cause decreasing spring recharge and runoff and increasing winter recharge and runoff (Waibel 2011, pp. 57-60; Mayer and Naman 2011, p. 3). However, there is spatial variation within the Deschutes sub-basins as to where the greatest increases in recharge and runoff will occur (Waibel 2011, pp. 57-60). Changes in seasonality of stream flows may be less affected by climate change along the crest of the Cascades in the upper watersheds of the Deschutes, Klamath, and Willamette River basins in Oregon, where many rivers receive groundwater recharge from subterranean aquifers and springs (Chang and Jones 2010, p. 107). Summer stream flows may thus be sustained in high Cascade basins that are groundwater fed (Chang and Jones 2010, p. 134). Conversely, Mayer and Naman (2011, p. 1) indicate that streamflow into Upper Klamath Lake will display absolute decreases in July-September base flows in groundwater basins as compared to surface-dominated basins. This earlier discharge of water in the spring will result in less streamflow in the summer (Mayer and Naman 2011, p. 12).

Although predictions of climate change impacts do not specifically address Oregon spotted frogs, short- and long-term changes in precipitation patterns and temperature regimes will likely affect wet periods, winter snow pack, and flooding events (Chang and Jones 2010). These changes are likely to affect amphibians through a variety of direct and indirect pathways, such as range shifts, breeding success, survival, dispersal, breeding phenology, availability and quality of aquatic habitats, food webs, competition, spread of diseases, and the interplay among these factors (Blaustein et al. 2010, entire; Hixon et al. 2010, p. 274; Corn 2003, entire). Amphibians have species-specific temperature tolerances, and exceeding these thermal thresholds is expected to reduce survival (Blaustein et al. 2010, pp. 286-287). Earlier spring thaws and warmer ambient temperatures may result in earlier breeding, especially at lower elevations in the mountains where breeding phenology is driven more by snow pack than by air temperature (Corn 2003, p. 624). Shifts in breeding phenology may also result in sharing breeding habitat with species not previously encountered and/or new competitive interactions and predator/prey dynamics (Blaustein et al. 2010, pp. 288, 294). Oregon spotted frogs are highly aquatic, and reductions in summer flows may result in summer habitat going dry, potentially resulting in increased mortality or forcing frogs to seek shelter in lower quality wetted areas where they are more susceptible to predation.

Amphibians are susceptible to many types of pathogens including trematodes, copepods, fungi, oomycetes, bacteria, and viruses. Changes in temperature and precipitation could alter host-pathogen interactions and/or result in range shifts resulting in either beneficial or detrimental impacts on the amphibian host (Blaustein et al. 2010, p. 296). Kiesecker et al. (2001a, p. 682) indicate climate change events, such as El Nino/Southern Oscillation, that result in less precipitation and reduced water depths at egg-laying sites results in high mortality of embryos because their exposure to UV-B and vulnerability to infection (such as Saprolegnia) is increased. Warmer temperatures and less freezing in areas occupied by bullfrogs is likely to increase bullfrog winter survivorship, thereby increasing the threat from predation. Uncertainty about climate change impacts does not mean that impacts may or may not occur; it means that the risks of a given impact are difficult to quantify (Schneider and Kuntz-Duriseti 2002, p. 54; Congressional Budget Office 2005, entire; Halsnaes et al. 2007, p. 129). Oregon spotted frogs occupy habitats at a wide range of elevations, and all of the occupied sub-basins are likely to experience precipitation regime shifts; therefore, the Oregon spotted frog's response to climate change is likely to vary across the range, and the population-level impacts are uncertain. The interplay between Oregon spotted frogs and their aquatic habitat will ultimately determine their population response to climate change. Despite the potential for future climate change throughout the range of the species, as discussed above, we have not identified, nor are we aware of any data on, an appropriate scale to evaluate habitat or population trends for the Oregon spotted frog or to make predictions about future trends and whether the species will be significantly impacted.

Conservation Efforts To Reduce Other Natural or Manmade Factors Affecting Its Continued Existence

The U.S. Department of Agriculture, Animal and Plant Health Inspection Service (APHIS), maintains voluntary agreements with private landowners concerning application of pesticides within the United States. Based on their 2010 operational procedures, all waterbodies (rivers, ponds, reservoirs, streams, vernal pools, wetlands, etc.) will be avoided by a minimum of a 50-foot buffer for ground application of bait, a 200-foot buffer for aerial application of bait, and a 500-foot buffer for the aerial application of liquids (USDA APHIS 2010, p. 4). As previously described under other threat factors, conservation efforts may also help reduce the threat of other natural or manmade factors affecting the species.

Summary of Other Natural or Manmade Factors

Many of the Oregon spotted frog breeding locations are small and isolated from other breeding locations. Moreover, due to their fidelity to breeding locations and vulnerability to fluctuating water levels, predation, and low overwinter survival, Oregon spotted frogs can experience rapid population turnovers that they may not be able to overcome. Genetic work indicates low genetic diversity within and high genetic differentiation among the six Oregon spotted frog groups identified by Blouin, and each of these groups has the signature of complete isolation with two groups showing indications of recent genetic drift. Poor water quality parameters and contaminants may act singly or in combination with other factors to result in inhibited fertilization and embryonic development, developmental anomalies, or reduced growth and survival. Oregon spotted frogs in every occupied sub-basin are subject to more than one stressor, such as loss or reduced quality of habitat and predation and, therefore, may be more susceptible to mortality and sublethal effects. The changing climate may exacerbate these stressors. Therefore, based on the best information available, we conclude that other natural or manmade factors are a threat to the Oregon spotted frog, which has significant population effects occurring throughout the entire (current) range of the species and these effects are expected to continue into the future.

Cumulative Effects From Factors A Through E

The Oregon spotted frog faces several threats, and all occupied sub-basins are subjected to multiple threats, which cumulatively pose a risk to individual populations (see Table 2, below). Many of these threats are intermingled, and the magnitude of the combined threats to the species is greater than the individual threats. For example, the small sizes and isolation of the majority of Oregon spotted frog breeding locations makes Oregon spotted frogs acutely vulnerable to fluctuating water levels, disease, predation, poor water quality, and extirpation from stochastic events. Hydrologic changes, resulting from activities such as water diversions and removal of beavers, increase the likelihood of fluctuating water levels and temperatures, and may also facilitate predators. Existing regulatory mechanisms facilitate hydrologic changes, and restoration actions are specifically designed to benefit salmonid species, which often results in the reduction of habitat quality and quantity for Oregon spotted frogs where they overlap.

Habitat management and a warming climate may improve conditions for pathogens and predators. Saprolegnia, Bd, and Ribeiroia ondatrae have been found in Oregon spotted frogs, and compounded with other stressors, such as UV-B exposure, degradation of habitat quality, or increased predation pressure, may contribute to population declines. Bd and R. ondatrae, in particular, infect post-metamorphic frogs and reductions in these life stages are more likely to lead to population declines. Sub-basins projected to transition from snow-dominant or transient to rain-dominant will be less susceptible to freezing temperatures with the expectation of reduced mortality of bullfrogs during winter and increased predation risk to Oregon spotted frogs.

Amphibian declines may frequently be associated with multiple correlated factors (Adams 1999, pp. 1167-1169). Two of the greatest threats to freshwater systems in western North America, exotic species and hydrological changes, are often correlated. In addition, occurrence and abundance of bullfrogs may be linked with invasions by nonnative fish (Adams et al. 2003, p. 349; Rowe and Garcia 2014, p. 147). Adams (1999) examined the relationships among introduced species, habitat, and the distribution and abundance of red-legged frogs in western Washington. Red-legged frog occurrence in the Puget lowlands was more closely associated with habitat structure and exotic fish than with the presence of bullfrogs (Adams 1999, pp. 1167-1168), and similar associations were found in a recent study in Oregon's Willamette Valley (Pearl et al. 2005b, p. 16). Rowe and Garcia (2014, p. 147) found native anuran counts were consistently lower in wetlands with nonnative fish, whereas bullfrog counts were higher. The spread of exotic species is correlated with a shift toward greater permanence in wetland habitats regionally (for example, Kentula et al. 1992, p. 115). For example, exotic fish and bullfrogs are associated with permanent wetlands. Conservation of more ephemeral wetland habitats, which directly benefit native amphibians such as Oregon spotted frogs, would be expected to reduce predation and competition threats posed by exotic fish and bullfrogs (Adams 1999, pp. 1169-1170; Rowe and Garcia 2014, p. 150). However, bullfrogs may be adapting because they have recently been found successfully breeding in ephemeral wetlands in the Willamette Valley, Oregon (Cook 2013, p. 656).

Amphibians are affected by complex interactions of abiotic and biotic factors, and are subjected simultaneously to numerous interacting stressors. For example, contaminants and UV-B radiation may result in mortality or induce sublethal effects on their own, but they may have synergistic, interaction effects that exceed the additive effects when combined. Some stressors, such as contaminants, may hamper the immune system, making amphibians more susceptible to pathogenic infections (Kiesecker 2002, p. 9902). Predator presence can alter the behavior of amphibians, resulting in more or less exposure to UV-B radiation (Michel and Burke 2011), thereby altering the rate of malformations. Climate-driven dry events that result in lower water levels may concentrate contaminants, as well as increase the amount of exposure to UV-B radiation. While any one of these individual stressors may not be a concern, a contaminant added to increased UV-B radiation exposure and a normally healthy population level of Ribeiroia ondatrae may lead to a higher mortality rate or an increased number of malformed frogs that exceeds the rate caused by any one factor alone (Blaustein et al. 2003, entire; Szurocksi and Richardson 2009 p. 382). Oregon spotted frogs in every occupied sub-basin are subject to more than one stressor and, therefore, may be more susceptible to mortality and sublethal effects.

The historical loss of Oregon spotted frog habitats and lasting anthropogenic changes in natural disturbance processes are exacerbated by the introduction of reed canarygrass, nonnative predators, and potentially climate change. In addition, current regulatory mechanisms and voluntary incentive programs designed to benefit fish species have inadvertently led to the continuing decline in quality of Oregon spotted frog habitats in some locations. The current wetland and stream vegetation management paradigm is generally a no-management or restoration approach that often results in succession to a tree- and shrub-dominated community that unintentionally degrades or eliminates remaining or potential suitable habitat for Oregon spotted frog breeding. Furthermore, incremental wetland loss or degradation continues under the current regulatory mechanisms. If left unmanaged, these factors are anticipated to result in the eventual elimination of remaining suitable Oregon spotted frog habitats or populations. The persistence of habitats required by the species is now largely management dependent.

Conservation efforts to ameliorate impacts from habitat degradation and predators are currently under way; however, the benefits of these conservation actions to Oregon spotted frogs are site-specific and do not counteract the impacts at a sub-basin scale. The cumulative effects of these threats are more than additive, and removing one threat does not ameliorate the others and may actually result in an increase in another threat. For example, removing livestock grazing to improve water quality—without continuing to manage the vegetation—can allow invasive reed canarygrass, trees, and shrubs to grow and effectively eliminate egg-laying habitat.

Therefore, based on the best scientific information available, we conclude that the cumulative effects from factors discussed in Factors A, C, and E, combined with the inadequacy of existing regulatory mechanisms discussed under Factor D, are a threat to the Oregon spotted frog, and these threats are significantly affecting populations throughout the entire range of the species. Moreover, these threats are expected to continue into the future.

Table 2—Threats Operating Within Each Sub-Basin *

Sub-basin	Factor A	Factor C	Factor E
Lower Fraser River	Wetland loss; hydrologic changes; development; grazing, reed canarygrass; water quality	Introduced warmwater fish; bullfrogs	Small population size; breeding locations disconnected; contaminants; cumulative effects of other threats; climate change.
Lower Chilliwack River	Grazing; reed canarygrass; water quality	Introduced warmwater fish	Small population size; breeding locations disconnected; contaminants; cumulative effects of other threats; climate change.
South Fork Nooksack	Grazing; reed canarygrass; shrub encroachment/planting; loss of beavers; water quality	Introduced coldwater fish	Small population size; cumulative effects of other threats; contaminants; climate change.
Samish River	Wetland loss; grazing; reed canarygrass; shrub encroachment/planting; water quality	Introduced warmwater fish; introduced coldwater fish	Breeding locations disconnected; contaminants; cumulative effects of other threats; climate change.
Black River	Wetland loss; reed canarygrass; shrub encroachment/planting; development; loss of beaver; water quality	Introduced warmwater fish; introduced coldwater fish; bullfrogs	Small population size; breeding locations disconnected; contaminants; cumulative effects of other threats; climate change.
White Salmon River	Wetland loss; reed canarygrass; water quality	Introduced coldwater fish	Cumulative effects of other threats; climate change.
Middle Klickitat River	Wetland loss; hydrologic changes; loss of beaver; development; grazing; reed canarygrass; shrub encroachment; water management	Introduced warmwater fish; introduced coldwater fish; bullfrogs	Cumulative effects of other threats; climate change.
Lower Deschutes	Shrub encroachment		Small population size; single occupied site within sub-basin; isolated from frogs in other sub-basins; cumulative effects of other threats; climate change.
Upper Deschutes	Wetland loss; reed canarygrass; shrub encroachment; hydrological changes (water management)	Introduced warmwater fish; introduced coldwater fish, bullfrogs	Breeding locations disconnected; cumulative effects of other threats; climate change.
Little Deschutes	Wetland loss; hydrological changes (water management); development; grazing; reed canarygrass; shrub encroachment	Introduced coldwater fish; bullfrogs	Breeding locations disconnected; cumulative effects of other threats; climate change.
McKenzie	Shrub encroachment	Introduced coldwater fish	Only two breeding locations in sub-basin, which are disconnected; cumulative effects of other threats; climate change.
Middle Fork Willamette	Shrub encroachment	Introduced coldwater fish	Single occupied site in sub-basin; disconnected from other sub-basins; cumulative effects of other threats; climate change.
Williamson	Development; grazing; shrub encroachment; loss of beaver	Introduced warmwater fish; introduced coldwater fish	Small population size; breeding locations disconnected; cumulative effects of other threats; climate change.
Upper Klamath Lake	Water management; development; shrub and reed canarygrass encroachment; grazing	Introduced warmwater fish; introduced coldwater fish; bullfrogs	Small population size; breeding locations disconnected; cumulative effects of other threats; climate change.
Upper Klamath	Wetland loss; water management; development; grazing; shrub encroachment; loss of beaver	Introduced warmwater fish; introduced coldwater fish	Small population size; breeding locations disconnected; cumulative effects of other threats; climate change.

Summary of Comments and Recommendations

In the proposed rule published on August 29, 2013 (78 FR 53582), we requested that all interested parties submit written comments on the proposal by October 28, 2013. On September 26, 2013 (78 FR 59334), we extended the comment period to November 12, 2013. We also contacted appropriate Federal and State agencies, scientific experts and organizations, and other interested parties and invited them to comment on the proposal. Newspaper notices inviting general public comment were published in The Olympian, the Yakima Herald Republic, The Goldendale Sentinel, The Bulletin, and the Mail Tribune. As also announced in that September 26, 2013, document, we held a public hearing in Lacey, Washington, on October 21, 2013. On September 18, 2013, we held an Oregon spotted frog workshop in Klamath Falls, Oregon, to provide the public with information on the species biology and distribution, and the listing and critical habitat rules. Public meetings were held in Sunriver and La Pine, Oregon, on December 3 and 4, 2013, respectively.

During the public comment period for the proposed rule, we received nearly 80 comment letters addressing the proposed listing for the Oregon spotted frog. During the October 21, 2013, public hearing, five individuals or organizations made comments on the proposed rule. All substantive information provided during the comment period has either been incorporated directly into this final determination or is addressed below.

Peer Review

In accordance with our peer review policy published on July 1, 1994 (59 FR 34270), we solicited expert opinion from nine knowledgeable individuals with scientific expertise that included familiarity with the Oregon spotted frog and its habitats, biological needs, and threats. We received responses from eight of the peer reviewers.

We reviewed all comments we received from the peer reviewers for substantive issues and new information regarding the listing of the Oregon spotted frog. All peer reviewers felt that the proposed rule was a thorough description of the status of the Oregon spotted frog and commented that they considered the proposed rule well researched and well written. Our requests for peer review are limited to a request for review of the merits of the scientific information in our documents; if peer reviewers have volunteered their personal opinions on matters not directly relevant to the science of our status assessment, we do not respond to those comments here. The peer reviewers provided a number of recommended technical corrections or edits to the proposed listing of the Oregon spotted frog. We evaluated and incorporated this information into this final rule when and where appropriate to clarify this final listing rule. Eight peer reviewers provided substantive comments on the proposed listing of the Oregon spotted frog, which we address below.

Comments From Peer Reviewers

(1) Comment: One peer reviewer thought the Service indicated that the reintroduction site at Joint Base Lewis McChord lacked suitable habitat and asked that we identify what features of the Oregon spotted frog's habitat were missing.

Our response: Our discussion concerning the lack of suitable habitat is in reference to the Nisqually River sub-basin where a number of historically occupied locations have been affected by development; we were not referring to the specific location of the reintroductions at Joint Base

Lewis-McChord military reservation, which may contain suitable habitat.

(2) Comment: One peer reviewer questioned our use of the sub-basin scale regarding the number of extant sites, rather than using a smaller scale, such as a 5th-field or 6th-field watershed. The reviewer was concerned that this may lead the reader to presume that it is the Service's implicit intention to retain occupancy at the scale of 4th fields.

Our response: We used the sub-basin scale to broadly summarize the distribution of the Oregon spotted frog. In Table 1, we have listed the historical and extant distribution of Oregon spotted frog throughout the range by sub-basin (4th field) and watershed (5th field), and in the Population Estimates and Status section we discussed the number of breeding locations found within each sub-basin. Additionally, when we constructed our threats matrix (Threats Synthesis Rangewide Analysis), we conducted our analysis at the 5th- and 6th-field scales and included a description of all known locations. We then summarized this information at the sub-basin scale in order to evaluate threats across the distribution of the species. The threats matrix was provided to peer reviewers and made available on both http://www.regulations.gov and the WFWO Web site.

(3) Comment: One peer reviewer questioned the exclusive use of the 2012 population estimates for Washington and suggested we include 2013 population estimates along with population estimates for other years for each of the monitored populations in order to demonstrate the annual variability in Oregon spotted frog estimates.

Our response: Annual variation in survey effort, area coverage, and timing at individual sites have led us to be cautious in comparing population estimates across years, and we have not relied upon them to determine trends, except where there was enough consistency between data sets to do so. The minimum population estimates were provided to give a general understanding of the number of frogs currently known in each sub-basin and the disparity between the 15 occupied sub-basins. The timing of the proposed rule and availability of data prohibited us from including 2013 survey data. We have updated the sub-basin information to include 2013 data where the new information expanded the distribution or significantly changed the minimum population estimate. In most cases, 2013 survey efforts were not as extensive as those conducted in 2011 and 2012, and, in some cases, the Service did not receive 2013 survey data. We have evaluated the 2013 data in our possession and determined that a change in status from the proposed rule is not warranted in any of the occupied sub-basins.

(4) Comment: Two peer reviewers questioned some aspects of our analysis of livestock grazing as a threat. Specifically, one peer reviewer asked us to categorize the effects of cattle grazing on Oregon spotted frog habitat into mesic and arid environments, breeding and non-breeding habitats, season, and cattle densities. In addition, this peer reviewer questioned our use of the term livestock, instead of cattle. Another peer reviewer stated that the personal opinions and biases of individual researchers contribute to seemingly contradictory conclusions about the compatibility of grazing with the well-being of the Oregon spotted frog and that speculation may be given more weight than deserved. In addition, this peer reviewer stated that some of the negative effects of grazing to Oregon spotted frog and its habitat that we discussed are not well supported by research or casual observation. These negative effects include the direct effect of mortality to adult frogs and eggs from trampling and numerous indirect effects to habitat, such as water contamination from urine and feces, increases in temperature and sediment production, alterations to stream morphology, effects on prey organisms, and changes to water quality.

Our response: We agree that the issue of grazing is controversial and the impacts have been posited to be both positive and negative. However, grazing and the potential impacts are not consistent across the range of the species. The weight of the evidence for other amphibian species and the negative impacts of grazing in riparian areas are well documented (see "Livestock

Grazing" section under Factor A discussion). Livestock as a whole break down banks and influence water quality if allowed unfettered access to waterbodies, and if livestock are in shallow water areas being used by frogs, trampling can occur. We agree that the term livestock can mean various animals domesticated so as to live and breed in a tame condition. We used the term livestock because at present we have information with specific regard to cattle and horses as grazers within Oregon spotted frog habitats.

There is little indication that categorizing the effects of grazing on Oregon spotted frogs in mesic versus arid environments would produce significantly different results. The purpose and intent of the grazing is what drives the effects of grazing. For example, if grazing is employed alongside other habitat management techniques as a method to maintain open water areas with short vegetation that is suitable for egg-laying where egg-laying habitat is a limiting factor, then some water quality degradation, trampling, and bank breakdown may be acceptable. However, this should not be taken to imply that there are no negative consequences associated with grazing as a habitat management technique. In cases where the primary objective of grazing is cattle production, the methods used may be different than those techniques employed to maintain or enhance Oregon spotted frog habitat. The goals, methods, and impacts to Oregon spotted frogs vary on a site-by-site basis. Our analysis considered both the possible positive and negative impacts of grazing but our final conclusion is that grazing presents a threat within the 10 occupied sub-basins where it currently occurs.

(5) Comment: One peer reviewer commented that our conclusion regarding malformations related to Planorbella snails was not adequately supported by the available data, stating that while trematode-caused malformations in frogs have been found to result in higher mortality rates than non-infected frogs, causing a negative effect at the individual level, effects at the population level are poorly understood.

Our response: We agree that the effects of these parasite-induced malformations on amphibians, including Oregon spotted frogs, are clear at the individual scale, but population-level effects remain largely uninvestigated. However, the viability of populations of pond-breeding amphibians is most vulnerable to losses of juveniles and adults when compared to losses of other life-history stages (Biek et al. 2002, p. 731). As these parasite-induced malformations primarily impact the survival of juveniles, it is logical to infer that where these parasites co-occur with Oregon spotted frogs and infect juveniles, the viability of Oregon spotted frog populations at those locations is likely to be negatively affected. We have amended our text to explain this conclusion. However, as indicated in Summary of Factors Affecting the Species, we have no information indicating that population declines in Oregon spotted frogs are occurring as a result of trematode-caused malformations. Disease continues to be a concern, but more information is needed to determine the severity of impact that diseases may have on Oregon spotted frogs. Therefore, under Factor C, we concluded that the best scientific information indicates that disease is not a threat to the Oregon spotted frog.

(6) Comment: One peer reviewer commented that our statements regarding water quality are using standards applied for human consumption and may not apply to the suitability of a waterbody to provide quality habitat for the Oregon spotted frog. He agreed with our statement that many Oregon streams do not meet the Oregon Department of Environmental Quality's water quality standards and believes this situation can be interpreted in at least two ways: That water quality is threatening frog populations in many Oregon streams, or that Oregon spotted frogs are capable of surviving and may in fact favor water quality conditions perceived to be poor by human standards.

Our response: We agree that not all water quality parameters are equal and the standards applied for humans may or may not be detrimental to Oregon spotted frogs. However, many of the parameters that we identified in association with water quality, such as pH and dissolved oxygen, are applicable, as is temperature when it results in algal blooms and low oxygen levels. Reduced water quality is documented in a number of occupied sub-basins (see Factor E discussion), and where this overlap occurs we consider poor water quality and contaminants to be threats to the Oregon spotted frog.

(7) Comment: One peer reviewer indicated the Oregon spotted frog's sensitivity to nitrate and nitrite, as presented by Marco et al. (1999), sounds alarming and recommended we revise the text. The peer reviewer also commented that the median lethal concentrations of nitrate and nitrite determined by Marco et al. (1999) was 1,000-fold the levels he observed in Oregon spotted frog breeding sites from grazing by cows at a dairy farm in Washington.

Our response: The maximum recommended level for nitrates in drinking water or for water containing warm-water fishes, as set by the EPA, exceeds the median lethal concentration for Oregon spotted frog larvae in laboratory studies, as documented by Marco et al. (1999, p. 2838), which was less than 10 mg/L. It is possible that waterways that do not exceed the drinking water quality standard could negatively impact Oregon spotted frogs; however, more field-based studies are needed to evaluate these impacts. Grazing is only one source of nitrates and nitrites; the EPA Web site lists the major sources of nitrates in drinking water to be runoff from fertilizer use, leaking from septic tanks and sewage, and erosion of natural deposits. Most currently known occupied sites for Oregon spotted frog are located in areas where residential septic tanks are used and farming practices include fertilizer application and grazing. We have revised the text in the water quality section to acknowledge the "maximum" levels as being toxic to amphibians and provided the maximum limits as set by EPA for human drinking water.

(8) Comment: One peer reviewer indicated our information regarding the number of breeding locations below the Wickiup Reservoir was inaccurate; we indicated there were four breeding areas, but the peer reviewer stated there were at least six.

Our response: In riverine wetlands along the Deschutes River below Wickiup Dam there are at least five known breeding locations, including a new location in La Pine State Park found in 2013. Dilman Meadow is within the Upper Deschutes River sub-basin but not along the Deschutes River below Wickiup Dam. The Crosswater population is included within the Little Deschutes River sub-basin, at the confluence of the Deschutes River. Language regarding the number and distribution of the known Oregon spotted frogs in the Upper Deschutes River sub-basin has been revised.

(9) Comment: One peer reviewer stated that while he agreed that most Oregon spotted frog populations are relatively small, isolated, and vulnerable to factors that may cause population extirpation, he did not believe that the listing proposal adequately supported climate change or contaminants as being significant threats.

Our response: In our proposed rule, we concluded that because Oregon spotted frogs occupy habitats at a wide range of elevations, and all of the occupied sub-basins are likely to experience precipitation regime shift, the Oregon spotted frog's response to climate change is likely to vary across the range and the population-level impacts are uncertain. We currently do not have the data to determine whether the species will be significantly impacted by climate change, and this final rule reflects that position. We reviewed our analysis in the proposed rule pertaining to threats associated with water quality and have revised our conclusion about the extent of this threat. Reduced water quality is documented in a number of occupied sub-basins, and where this overlap occurs we consider poor water quality and contaminants to be threats to the Oregon spotted frog.

(10) Comment: One peer reviewer indicated that we should have included the potential threat from manmade barriers to seasonal movements by Oregon spotted frogs because these barriers may

prevent frog movement to and from breeding sites or other habitats.

Our response: We agree with the peer reviewer that these manmade barriers could pose a threat to local populations. In Washington, impassable culverts have been identified as an issue in relation to migration of salmon species to or from spawning habitat. Among the culverts identified by Washington Department of Transportation (WSDOT) in relation to a lawsuit involving salmon migration, only four come within 500 ft (153 m) of areas identified as occupied by the Oregon spotted frog. Two of these occur in the Samish River sub-basin and two in the South Fork Nooksack River sub-basin. All four of these are on tributaries that are not known to be used by Oregon spotted frogs and that are not known to occur between potential breeding habitat and summer/dry season habitat. Therefore, it does not appear that the culverts identified under this process pose a threat to Oregon spotted frogs. However, outside of salmon migration areas in Washington and throughout Oregon, we do not have the information to evaluate the number and distribution of manmade barriers; thus at this time, we are unable to evaluate the severity of this threat. We have added text to the "Hydrological Changes" section under the Factor A discussion in this rule to reflect the potential of manmade barriers to hinder frog movement.

(11) Comment: One peer reviewer pointed out that our statement regarding the potential for hydrologic connectivity and movement between populations in the Klamath Lake populations does not take into consideration the potential for Oregon spotted frogs to move during flood events, through the extensive ditch system within the Wood River Valley, or between the west side and east side breeding complexes. In addition, the peer reviewer pointed out that while the sample size was small, Robertson's and Funk's (2012) reported evidence of gene flow between the Wood River and Fourmile Creek indicates that there is movement between populations on the west and east sides of the Wood River Valley.

Our response: While there is evidence of some genetic exchange between the west (Fourmile Creek) and east (Wood River) sides of Upper Klamath Lake, Robertson and Funk (2012, p. 5) indicate the sampling sites within the two clusters (H and I) are geographically isolated, indicating limited mixing among sites. Genetic exchange is extremely low beyond 6 mi (10 km) (Blouin et al. 2010, pp. 2186, 2188), and the closest distance between currently known breeding areas in Fourmile Creek and Wood River is greater than 4 mi. Movement by Oregon spotted frogs during high water events would not constitute a true hydrologic connection that enables regular or semi-regular dispersal across the Upper Klamath Lake. High water events are unlikely to frequently connect these areas due to roads and dikes that separate these two areas. Additionally, the intersecting area is mostly comprised of ranch land and water typically does not enter the area due to manipulation of water levels. Therefore, we continue to consider the sites in the Upper Klamath Lake sub-basin to be isolated.

(12) Comment: One peer reviewer indicated the 2012 egg mass counts at Maria Slough in British Columbia increased over those conducted in previous years, suggesting the apparent decline in the mid-2000s may have been attributable to a population cycle and/or the result of excessive flooding in some years that reduced suitable breeding sites in those years. The reviewer recommended we revise the status from "declining" to "likely stable" and suggested that the Maria Slough population is probably exhibiting typical high and low population cycles often seen in amphibian populations.

Our response: While we agree that amphibian populations may exhibit typical high and low cycles, which can be attributed to a wide variety of factors, such as extreme flooding or low-water events that limit egg-laying locations, the Oregon spotted frog population at Maria Slough has been supplemented over many years with frogs through the captive rearing program and these frogs were expected to mature to breeding age in 2010-2011 (COSEWIC 2011, p. 32). This supplementation may account for the increase in egg mass numbers in 2012. We have determined that the recent increases in egg mass counts do not warrant a change in population status to that of "stable" given an estimated 28 percent likelihood of Oregon spotted frogs inhabiting the site by 2050 (COSEWIC 2011, p. 32).

(13) Comment: One peer reviewer cautioned that inference drawn from many Oregon spotted frog life-history studies should not be extrapolated globally due to the tendency for these studies to be site-specific and not representative of site-to-site variation.

Our response: We agree that caution should be exercised in using site-specific data; to address this concern the information presented in the life history section describes the variation across the range (latitude and elevation), including British Columbia south to the Klamath Basin. Many of the references used in the Life History section of this rule represent syntheses of information, such as McAllister and Leonard 1997, Leonard et al. 1993, and Hayes 1994. Within the Summary of Factors Affecting the Species section, we used the best available information. In many cases the response by frogs to a stressor is not widely studied, and the results must be extrapolated across the range. While stressors will vary across the range of the species, it is reasonable to assume that the response will not; therefore we have applied our best professional judgment where it has been necessary to bridge the gap.

(14) Comment: One peer reviewer suggested we acknowledge uncertainty around the egg mass counts representing a count of adults. He provided one anecdotal observation of a female caught in a spawned out condition that was followed and recaptured several weeks later and was described on the capture form as gravid and appearing to be ready to lay another clutch.

Our response: Phillipsen et al. (2009, p. 7) found that Oregon spotted frogs in their study area conformed to the assumption that a female lays only one egg mass per season. However, we have revised the text to include the additional uncertainty regarding the number of clutches per female per year.

(15) Comment: One peer reviewer commented that we had not made it clear how the assumed loss of historical range (up to 90 percent of the species' former range) was used in our listing determination and believed that multiple references to the estimated loss of the historical range may mislead the reader by implying that the range loss itself constitutes a threat.

Our response: The estimate of historical range loss is referenced in several places in this rule and is presented to explain to the reader the extent of the loss of the species across its historical range. Additionally, our evaluation of the historical threats to the Oregon spotted frog informs our analysis of the species' response to current or future threats as summarized under Summary of Factors Affecting the Species. In the Determination section, we synthesize our evaluation of past, present, and future threats to the Oregon spotted frog in order to determine whether the species warrants listing based on current and future threats.

(16) Comment: One peer reviewer asked whether recreation should be considered a threat and gave examples of having observed indiscriminate amphibian egg mass collection and random shooting of frogs by members of the public.

Our response: In Washington, only one area (Trout Lake Creek) experiences recreational use due to nearby Federal and private campgrounds. Most Federal and State lands within currently known Oregon spotted frog areas have limited access. Most other occupied lands are privately owned. Oregon spotted frogs are a cryptic species, staying near and in the water and diving under vegetation to take cover when disturbed. Therefore, they are seen less often than most species, which reduces the likelihood for collection or killing of adults, though their egg masses may be vulnerable where broad public access occurs in conjunction with breeding sites. Recreation has not been identified as a threat to the frog in the Deschutes Basin; although Oregon spotted frogs occur within lakes and rivers that receive recreational use on National Forests in this basin, there is limited access to the marshes inhabited by the frog. In the Klamath Basin area of Oregon, recreation is not known to be threat. We note the peer reviewer's concerns, but have no other information that would lead us to determine that recreation may be a threat to the species.

Comments From States

Section 4(i) of the Act states, "the Secretary shall submit to the State agency a written justification for [her] failure to adopt regulations consistent with the agency's comments or petition." Comments we received from States regarding the proposal to list the Oregon spotted frog are addressed below. We received comments from WDFW, WDNR, WSDOT, WDOE, and Oregon State Department of Transportation related to biological information, threats, and the inadequacy of regulatory mechanisms. The agencies provided a number of recommendations for technical corrections or edits to the proposed listing of the Oregon spotted frog. We have evaluated and incorporated this information where appropriate to clarify this final rule. In instances where the Service may have disagreed with an interpretation of the technical information that was provided, we have responded to the State directly.

(17) Comment: We received requests from several State agencies as well as from public commenters about the development of a rule under section 4(d) of the Act to provide incidental take exemptions for various activities. The activities for which coverage was requested include: Irrigation district activities; grazing; agricultural diversions and drainage; groundwater pumping; agricultural activities; road maintenance; dredging of ditches; vegetation management; development; stormwater management; habitat restoration; research; and monitoring.

Our response: Whenever any species is listed as a threatened species, the Service may develop a rule under section 4(d) of the Act that exempts take under certain conditions. This exemption from take under a 4(d) rule could include provisions that are tailored to the specific conservation needs of the threatened species and may be more or less restrictive than the general prohibitive provisions detailed at 50 CFR 17.31.

We considered the development of a 4(d) rule that would exempt take of Oregon spotted frogs when that take was incidental to implementing State, regional, or local comprehensive Oregon spotted frog conservation programs. We also considered exempting all activities and efforts conducted by individual landowners on non-Federal lands that are consistent with maintaining or advancing the conservation of Oregon spotted frog, but fall outside of a more structured conservation plan. We further considered exemption from take on lands that are managed following technical guidelines that have been determined by the Service to provide a conservation benefit to the Oregon spotted frog, such as the mowing of reed canarygrass. We requested specific information that would provide us a high level of certainty that such a program would lead to the long-term conservation of Oregon spotted frogs (see Consideration of a 4(d) Special Rule in the August 29, 2013, proposed listing rule).

Although we received several requests for activities to include in a 4(d) rule, except as noted below, we did not receive specific information such as technical guidelines or conservation plans that may have allowed us to determine that a 4(d) rule exempting take for those activities would be necessary and advisable to provide a conservation benefit to the Oregon spotted frog. Some of the activities, such as irrigation, grazing, agricultural diversions, groundwater pumping (hydrologic changes), development, and certain vegetation management methods, for which consideration of a 4(d) rule was requested, are primary threats to the continued existence of the species. We did not receive specific information from requesters that would allow us to determine that a 4(d) rule for these activities would provide a conservation benefit to the Oregon spotted frog; therefore, an exception to the prohibition of take of the species due to these activities is not appropriate. For many of these activities, incidental take is more appropriately addressed through the development of a habitat conservation plan (HCP) or, if a Federal nexus exists, through consultation with the Service under section 7 of the Act. Other activities, such as haying and some vegetation management methods (such as mowing of reed canarygrass or installation of barrier cloth), are not anticipated to result in take of the Oregon spotted frog if these activities include appropriate conservation measures and occur when frogs are not known to be present; therefore, consideration of a 4(d) rule exempting incidental take for these activities is not necessary. Additionally, management activities vary greatly across the range of the species, and without specific technical guidelines or conservation plans we are unable to determine the conservation value of these activities to the Oregon spotted frog.

We received technical guidelines pertaining to road maintenance; associated roadside vegetation management; and ditch, culvert, and stormwater pond maintenance activities in Washington. However, we are aware that because a federal nexus exists for some of these activities, they will be covered, as appropriate, under a future programmatic section 7 consultation. Also, in most cases, the stormwater ponds mentioned are disconnected from permanent water sources, and we are not aware of Oregon spotted frogs using these types of ponds; therefore, no take is expected. Based on the information provided by the WSDOT, there is very little overlap between their activities and Oregon spotted frogs. As described, their activities could be either beneficial or detrimental to Oregon spotted frogs, and these activities would be better addressed through other conservation tools, such as section 7 consultation or HCPs. We will continue to work with the WSDOT and counties to determine the most appropriate coverage for activities that will not be covered under section 7 consultation.

We also received a request for a 4(d) rule from the Oregon Department of Transportation based on their "Routine Road Maintenance: Water Quality and Habitat Guide Best Management Practices." The best management practices (BMPs) found in these guidelines for aquatic species are specific to Pacific salmon and steelhead. Although these BMPs avoid and minimize adverse effects to aquatic systems to the extent practicable, there are no specific criteria to protect amphibians. For example, the BMPs for beaver dam removal would need to be modified because Oregon spotted frogs can be dependent on beaver activity to create and maintain suitable habitat. We would like to work with the Oregon Department of Transportation to incorporate BMPs that will avoid and minimize impacts to the Oregon spotted frog.

The Deschutes County Roads Department also submitted comments requesting a 4(d) rule for road maintenance and operations, including BMPs for facilities within or near riparian areas. We did not receive specific information on the County's BMPs that would allow us to determine that a 4(d) rule for these activities would provide a conservation benefit to Oregon spotted frog. Therefore, we will continue to work with the Deschutes County Road Department to evaluate these activities and determine the most appropriate tool for coverage under the Act.

We also received a comment from the Deschutes Basin Board of Control requesting a 4(d) rule; we address their comments later, under Comment (50).

Based on the information above, we have not proposed a rule under section 4(d) of the Act for the Oregon spotted frog, and the general provisions at 50 CFR 17.31 will apply. Additionally, the normal take provisions provided by section 17.31(b) of the Act to State conservation agencies operating a conservation program pursuant to the terms of a cooperative agreement with the Service in accordance with section 6(c) of the Act will apply.

We may continue to consider developing a proposed 4(d) rule after this listing is finalized if we were to receive appropriate specific information that would provide us with a high level of certainty that such activities would lead to the long-term conservation of Oregon spotted frogs.

(18) Comment: WDFW asserted that our statement indicating that there has been little survey effort in California since 1996 is incorrect. The commenter indicated that the USGS out of Point Reyes and the USFS group out of Humboldt State University have done extensive surveys in northeastern California, including a number which were conducted after 1996, and some of which overlap the historic range of the Oregon spotted frog.

Our response: In response to this comment, we contacted staff at Humboldt State University and USGS at Point Reyes. We confirm that surveys have been completed in northeastern California, but neither group encountered Oregon spotted frogs during their survey work. However, extensive surveys have not been conducted, and, therefore, we cannot confirm that Oregon spotted frogs are extirpated in California.

(19) Comment: WDFW suggested that more emphasis needed to be placed on the benefits that moderate controlled grazing can have on Oregon spotted frog habitat, stating that grazing is most likely to be a benefit and could be employed as an important tool across western Washington and British Columbia, Canada, where reed canarygrass achieves problematic densities.

Our response: While we examined both the potential positive and negative effects of livestock grazing, we concluded that grazing is not uniformly beneficial across the range of the Oregon spotted frog. Please see our response to Comment (4).

(20) Comment: WDOE suggested that text in the proposed rule appears to confuse the Sumas River in Whatcom County, Washington, with the Chilliwack River in British Columbia, Canada. The commenter asserted that in one part of the rule the Sumas River is described as a tributary to the Lower Chilliwack River watershed, which the commenter believed to be correct, but pointed out that elsewhere in the rule the Sumas River was used interchangeably with the Chilliwack River and/or the Lower Chilliwack River, which the commenter felt was incorrect.

Our response: The confusion arises from the multiple geographic scales used in this rule. The section entitled "Current Range/Distribution" summarized data at the 4th field sub-basin scale, except for Washington, where Oregon spotted frogs are currently distributed in only one 5th-field watershed within the six occupied sub-basins. The Sumas River is a tributary to the Lower Chilliwack River watershed (5th field) and to the Fraser River sub-basin (4th field). Because we are considering the species across its range, we attempted to use a consistent naming convention across the range. We have made changes to the text of this rule to more clearly identify the Sumas River as tributary to the Lower Chilliwack River watershed and the Fraser River sub-basin.

(21) Comment: WDOE indicated that our statement under Factor D, Local Laws and Regulations, regarding shoreline setbacks and impervious surfaces in Whatcom County was incorrect.

Our response: We referred to the Whatcom County SMP, Table 23.90.13.C, which provides the setbacks for a variety of activities. The setbacks may be as little as 5 ft; however, in the areas where Oregon spotted frogs are known to occur in the county, the land designations are primarily rural, resource, conservancy, or natural, and the setbacks in these areas begin at 15 ft (Whatcom County SMP 2008, pp. 96-99). The impervious surface allowance of 10 percent is also included in this table.

(22) Comment: WDNR stated that the proposed listing of the Oregon spotted frog presents a potential conflict between the long-term Washington State Forest Practices Rules and their

associated HCP, citing a misalignment between management strategies for wetlands and riparian areas and the habitat maintenance and enhancement needs for the Oregon spotted frog. Because the Oregon spotted frog is not a covered species under the Forest Practices HCP and the proposed listing decision does not draw a specific determination regarding the potential for incidental take of the species while conducting forest management activities covered by the Forest Practices HCP, the regulating State agency expressed its desire to avoid a circumstance where actions approved to benefit one set of listed species may potentially adversely impact another listed species.

Our response: Oregon spotted frog, as a species, is not generally dependent on a forested landscape; therefore there is a lower likelihood that Oregon spotted frogs or their habitat will be negatively affected by forest management activities. That said, Oregon spotted frogs may occur in areas delineated as forested wetlands (e.g., along Trout Lake Creek) or downstream from forest management activities, and management agencies should be aware of the activities that may negatively impact them. An example of such activity may include upslope management activities that alter the hydrology of streams, springs, or wetlands upon which Oregon spotted frogs depend. Activities that are currently allowed under the Forest Practices HCP may impact Oregon spotted frogs or their habitat. Conversely, disallowing management actions that could improve habitat for Oregon spotted frogs may be detrimental. For example, a lack of options to manage trees and/or shrubs that encroach into the wetlands may reduce the availability of suitable egg-laying habitat. We wish to highlight that some management of riparian areas under the Forest Practices HCP may or may not result in incidental take of Oregon spotted frogs, depending on the timing. For example, incidental take would not be anticipated for tree or shrub removal conducted during the dry season. We also note that areas of concern are limited to a very small subset of lands included or covered under the Forest Practices HCP. If there is a process for landowners to obtain a variance from WDNR in order to re-establish or enhance Oregon spotted frog habitat, the Service recommends that WDNR make that process available to willing landowners. Otherwise, the Service recommends WDNR consider its options for obtaining incidental take coverage for its Forest Practice Permit process.

Public Comments

(23) Comment: One commenter expressed concern about the availability of unpublished reports in the development of the rule.

Our response: The Service receives and uses information on the biology, ecology, distribution, abundance, status, and trends of species from a wide variety of sources as part of our responsibility to implement the Act. To assure the quality of the biological, ecological, and other information used by the Service in our implementation of the Act, it is the policy of the Service (59 FR 34271; July 1, 1994) to require biologists to evaluate all scientific and other information that will be used to support listing actions to ensure that information used is reliable, credible, and represents the best scientific and commercial data available. Supporting documentation we used in preparing the proposed rule was available for public inspection on http://www.regulations.gov, or at the U.S. Fish and Wildlife Service, Washington Fish and Wildlife Office (see FOR FURTHER INFORMATION CONTACT). Instructions for how to gain access to this information was provided in the August 29, 2013, proposed rule.

(24) Comment: Three commenters expressed concerns that the listing of the Oregon spotted frog would result in changes to mosquito abatement, specifically along the Deschutes River. Two of the commenters believe that managing local water resources to increase the wetlands for the Oregon spotted frog would result in greater numbers of mosquitos and would create a potential public health risk attributable to mosquito-borne encephalitic disease (West Nile virus).

Conversely, the third commenter suggested that an extinction of the Oregon spotted frog would increase the potential for insect overpopulation, causing further disruption to the ecosystem and effectively endangering other vulnerable species.

Our response: Mosquito control continues to occur in the Deschutes River area, specifically through application of the biological control agent Bti. Studies indicate Bti typically does not significantly affect vertebrates (Siegel et al. 1987, p. 723; Merritt et al. 1989; pp. 408-410; Hanowski et al. 1997, entire; Niemi et al. 1999, entire; Siegel 2001, entire), including amphibians (multiple studies synthesized in Glare and O'Callaghan 1998, pp. 24, 28). However, indirect effects may occur through reduction of food (insects) (Hanowski et al. 1997; Niemi et al. 1999, entire; Mercer et al. 2005, p. 692). The Service considers these potential indirect effects on the Oregon spotted frog to be negligible, considering the breadth of the Oregon spotted frog's diet and the specificity of the mosquito abatement treatments employed, which primarily affects the larvae of nematoceran ("thread-horned") flies (the group that includes mosquitos). At this time, we do not anticipate changes to the mosquito control program using Bti. Should more or newer information relating specifically to direct or indirect impacts on Oregon spotted frogs become available in the future, the Service will revisit this issue. We have updated the Background section of this rule to include a short discussion of the indirect effects of Bti and methoprene on the Oregon spotted frog.

(25) Comment: Two commenters specifically requested close collaboration between the Service and the USFS to ensure timely conservation of the Oregon spotted frog on USFS lands through the revision of already existing projects, and development of standards, guidelines, or management plans.

Our response: The Service coordinates and provides technical assistance to other Federal agencies, including the USFS, on a broad scope of work. The USFS has been proactive in developing site management plans specific to Oregon spotted frogs. Development of forest plans, land use classifications, standards and guidelines, and project planning remains under the purview of the Federal agencies developing such products. If a Federally authorized, funded, or conducted action could affect a listed species or its critical habitat, the responsible Federal agency is then required to enter into consultation with the Service under section 7 of the Act.

(26) Comment: A representative of Modoc County, California, asserted that the Service failed to follow Federal procedures when publishing the proposal to list the Oregon spotted frog. The commenter cited case law determining that the Service is required to give actual notice to local government of its intent to propose a species for listing.

Our response: Under 16 U.S.C. 1533(b)(5)(A)(ii), the Secretary is required to provide actual notice of the proposed regulation to each county in which the species is believed to occur. The Oregon spotted frog is not currently known or believed to occur in either Modoc or Siskiyou Counties; therefore, the Service did not provide notification to these counties.

(27) Comment: One commenter suggested that more attention be given to the extent of the historical range of the Oregon spotted frog and requested an evaluation of the factors likely contributing to the demise of historical populations as a way to become informed about the factors affecting the remaining populations.

Our response: Historical location information is presented in this rule to give the reader perspective on the decline of the species, but a listing analysis is focused on the current distribution and the threats to those populations. In many of the historically occupied watersheds, the specific location information necessary to determine why Oregon spotted frogs may no longer occur there is unavailable, but can reliably be attributed to human development. The effects of towns, homes, or infrastructure for both human habitation and for agriculture have resulted in the loss of suitable habitat in many of the historically occupied watersheds (for example, the Green River/Lake Washington area in Washington). While we agree that evaluating reasons for loss in historically occupied areas may inform ways to recover the species, the purpose of this evaluation is to determine the threats facing the currently occupied areas.

(28) Comment: Two commenters suggested that unidentified occupied locations may exist for Oregon spotted frog—one because a handful of such sites were documented as recently as 2011 and 2012, the other because of a 1991 document suggesting that additional surveys be conducted on the east side of the Cascade mountain range. In addition, one of the commenters asserted that the Service does not have any credible data regarding Oregon spotted frog populations on private lands adjoining the Conboy Lake NWR.

Our response: The information provided by the Service in the Current Range/Distribution section includes the newly identified watersheds and the one reintroduction project. All of these locations are within the historical range (i.e., Puget Trough) of the Oregon spotted frog. While we continue to survey for Oregon spotted frogs in potentially suitable habitat, both in historically and non-historically occupied sub-basins, we cannot speculate as to whether additional populations may occur. In addition, our analysis for listing purposes is based on the status and threats according to the best scientific and commercial data available, including occurrence records.

Subsequent to the 1991 document cited by the commenter, the Oregon spotted frog and Columbia spotted frog were separated into two species (see Taxonomy section). In Washington, frogs in the higher elevations near the Cascade crest (both east and west) have been identified as Cascades frogs and in the lower elevations on the east side of the Cascade Crest as Columbia spotted frogs.

While specific survey information does not exist for the private lands adjoining Conboy Lake NWR, the habitat for the Oregon spotted frog does not stop at the boundaries of the refuge. Due to the contiguous nature of the known occupied habitat on the refuge with the habitat on the adjoining private lands, the Service considers the adjoining lands occupied.

(29) Comment: One commenter believed we were inconsistent in our application of the status of the Oregon spotted frog occupied sub-basins. We denoted the Lower Fraser River and Middle Klickitat sub-basins as declining and White Salmon River sub-basin as having no determinable trend because numbers may be rebounding in portions of the Trout Lake area. The commenter believes we should not have concluded that the Middle Klickitat sub-basin was declining because of a similarity to the White Salmon River sub-basin.

Our response: One of the challenges in developing a listing determination for a species that spans multiple States is that scientific and monitoring data are often collected according to the methods preferred by individual researchers, rather than under a standard protocol. Results from some data collection methods can be compared to results from other methods through bridging studies, but some results are not comparable. Where we have no supported way to make comparisons between the results from differing data collection methods, we may not be able to draw conclusions, even if the data look similar. Based on the best data available, evidence indicates there is a declining trend in the Middle Klickitat River sub-basin (Hayes and Hicks 2011, entire; Hallock 2013, p. 36). There is no equivalent evidence available for the Trout Lake area (Hallock 2012) that indicates there are areas within the Middle Klickitat River sub-basin that are rebounding.

(30) Comment: One commenter asserted that the Service estimate for the number of Oregon spotted frogs in Upper Deschutes River and Little Deschutes River sub-basins (3,530 and 6,628 breeding adults, respectively) indicates that each population is of considerable size and viability and highlighted the co-existence of these populations in areas where human activity, such as

irrigation water storage, release, diversion, and return, has been prevalent for more than a century.

Our response: The Service does not consider the minimum population estimates in the Upper Deschutes River or Little Deschutes River sub-basins to constitute a population of "considerable size and viability." Franklin (1980) proposed the 50/500 rule, whereby an effective population size (N_e) of 50 is required to prevent unacceptable rates of inbreeding and an N_e of 500 is required to ensure overall genetic variability. Phillipsen et al. (2010) compared the adult Oregon spotted frog census population (N = 428) from a breeding site near Sunriver, Oregon, to the effective population size (N_e = 36.7) with the result of N_e/N = 0.086, which fell within the general range of DNA-based estimates for ranid frogs (Phillipsen et al. 2010, p. 742). Application of the 50/500 rule provides that an Oregon spotted frog population of greater than 581 breeding adults (N/N_e = 50/.086) at the Sunriver breeding site would be required to prevent inbreeding depression and a population of 5,814 breeding adults (N/N_e = 500/.086) would be required for a high probability of survival over time. Thus, the minimum population estimate for the Upper Deschutes River sub-basin (3,530) is considerably less than the population needed for only one site, Sunriver (5,814). Therefore, the Service does not consider the current Upper Deschutes River sub-basin's Oregon spotted frog populations to be of adequate size or viability.

Within the Little Deschutes River sub-basin, most of these breeding adults are confined to one area, Big Marsh (5,324 out of 6,628), which is not subject to irrigation district activities. We stated that the trend at Big Marsh appears to be increasing; however, there are no trend data available for the remainder of the sub-basin. Therefore, our determination of an undetermined trend for this sub-basin is accurate.

We agree that the Oregon spotted frogs in the Upper Deschutes River and the Little Deschutes River sub-basins continue to be present within areas of regulated flow associated with irrigation district activities for more than a century. However, without the irrigation district activities, the Oregon spotted frog populations in these sub-basins may be higher in number and better distributed throughout the sub-basin.

(31) Comment: One commenter believes the Service lacks sufficient evidence to establish that the Oregon spotted frog should be listed as a threatened species. The commenter stated that while the Service asserts that data show the frog is disappearing from its historical range, the Service admits that it has not studied population trend data in 13 of 15 sub-basins where the frog is known to occur. Therefore, the commenter claims that the Service has based its proposed listing decision not on substantial evidence of frog decline, but on absence of evidence countering a presumption of decline.

Our response: The Service is not required to show that a species is in decline in order to make a determination that it is threatened. A listing determination is an assessment of the best scientific and commercial information available regarding the past, present, and future threats to the Oregon spotted frog. While the loss of Oregon spotted frog across the historical distribution and the status of the species within its current range is considered in this assessment, the majority of the assessment is focused on the ongoing and future threats to the species within the currently occupied areas. All of the known Oregon spotted frog occupied sub-basins are currently affected by one or more threats. The immediacy, severity, and scope of these threats are such that the Oregon spotted frog is likely to become endangered throughout all or a significant portion of its range within the foreseeable future.

(32) Comment: One commenter suggested that the proposed listing rule should reassess the role shrubs play in support of beaver re-establishment in each frog sub-basin, since beaver re-establishment will affect both tree encroachment and succession to a tree-dominated community. The commenter noted that if a proper hydrologic regime were restored and maintained, plant

communities that provide frog habitat would not succeed to tree-dominated communities.

Our response: We acknowledge that shrubs are an important component for maintaining beaver habitat, but highlight the threat posed by succession to a tree- and/or shrub-dominated community where natural disturbances processes (such as beavers, flooding, and fire) have been or continue to be removed. We are especially concerned about wetland and riparian areas that provide egg-laying habitat that is being actively planted with willows and other riparian shrubs in order to cool water temperatures for salmonids. These actions can degrade or eliminate the shallow open-water conditions necessary for egg laying. We do not advocate for shrub removal throughout areas inhabited by Oregon spotted frogs, especially where they support beavers, but where natural disturbance processes are lacking, succession to shrub- and then tree-dominated communities will continue to pose a threat.

(33) Comment: Two commenters stated that the use of the term "early seral vegetation" to represent egg-laying habitat was not supported and does not conform to seral stages of plant communities of riparian areas and wetlands at cited in Kovalchik (1987) and Crowe et al. (2004). In addition, the commenters suggested that too much disturbance can force wetland communities toward drier plant associations, which may not favor Oregon spotted frogs.

Our response: Our use of the term "early seral" in the proposed listing rule was intended to convey the idea of non-forested areas in early stages of succession. Use of the term "late seral" to represent a wetland that is in a "stable state" where change in the vegetation is minimal over time is indeed accurate when applied to an intact wetland ecosystem, but may be confusing to those who may equate the term "late seral" to "older forest." We note that Oregon spotted frogs do not currently occur in intact stable wetland ecosystems throughout the majority of their range; they occur in systems that have been modified by humans such that the normal disturbance processes have been lost and succession to trees and shrubs is occurring. We agree that classification of the Oregon spotted frog as an early seral-dependent species is not entirely accurate, but note here that the vegetation at egg-laying areas in at least 7 of the 15 occupied sub-basins currently consists of reed canarygrass, not native wetland species. Maintenance of the appropriate vegetation height and water depth necessary for egg laying within these areas is crucial to the persistence of Oregon spotted frogs in these sub-basins. In this rule, we have revised the language in the Background and Summary of Factors Affecting the Species sections, where appropriate, to remove the term "early seral." We highlight that vegetation succession or encroachment into breeding sites for Oregon spotted frog constitute a threat to the species.

(34) Comment: One commenter asserted that the threat from grazing was understated in the proposed rule and suggested a more detailed discussion of the impacts grazing has on frog habitats is needed.

Our response: The best information available on grazing in areas occupied by Oregon spotted frog indicates there are both negative and positive impacts. We believe we evaluated the best available scientific information and provided a balanced summary of both the negative and positive impacts under the "Livestock Grazing" section of the Factor A discussion and that the full extent of the negative impacts have been evaluated. For further information, please see our response to Comment (4).

(35) Comment: Two commenters wrote regarding water management and drastic draw-downs below the Wickiup Reservoir in the Upper Deschutes sub-basin that have resulted in fish kills. These commenters indicated the Oregon Water Resources Department dewaters the Upper Deschutes River annually in the fall and expressed concern at the lack of Service involvement to protect animals under our jurisdiction.

Our response: The Service does not have direct regulatory authority over the water management within the Deschutes River Basin. By law, all surface and ground water in Oregon belongs to the public, and the Oregon Water Resources Department is the public State-level agency charged with administration of the laws governing surface and ground water resources, including the protection of existing water rights. Much of the river water within the Deschutes River was allocated long ago and, as such, is subject to the laws governing water rights. If a Federally authorized, funded, or conducted action may affect a listed species or its critical habitat, the responsible Federal agency must enter into consultation with the Service under section 7 of the Act. However, where there is no Federal nexus, State laws govern water management. With this final rule, however, the Act's prohibitions will apply to all activities that harm Oregon spotted frogs, and we expect to work with landowners to develop habitat conservation plans that address those activities.

(36) Comment: One commenter stated that the proposed rule suggests nonnative predators are transferred via the pumping of groundwater. Another commenter believed the proposed rule did not adequately weight the importance of groundwater resources to the persistence of Oregon spotted frog and felt the proposed rule should have included an assessment of the threats to groundwater, due to the contributions it makes to the maintenance of Oregon spotted frog habitat.

Our response: There is no biological information that suggests nonnative predators are transferred via groundwater pumping, and the proposed rule did not state or intend to imply there was such a threat. The final rule remains consistent with this original position.

The Service agrees that there is need to protect groundwater resources, as many wetland habitats occupied by Oregon spotted frogs are supported by groundwater. Pumping of groundwater can result in lower water levels in groundwater systems, diminished flow of springs, and reduced streamflow (Gannett et al. 2007, pp. 59-60, 65), but the extent of groundwater pumping effects to streamflow within Oregon spotted frog sub-basins and its impact on Oregon spotted frogs is currently unclear (Gannett et al. 2007, p. 65). In the Upper and Little Deschutes River sub-basins, the analysis of groundwater changes discussed in Gannett et al. (2013) is difficult to correlate directly with impacts to Oregon spotted frog. There is a scarcity of hydrologic gauges in certain parts of the occupied sub-basins, and there are only five well-testing locations upstream of Bend, Oregon, in proximity to areas occupied by Oregon spotted frog. Although the Little Deschutes River sub-basin experienced groundwater level declines since 2000, Gannett et al. (2013) stated that wells in the "La Pine sub-basin south of Bend" tend to respond to climate cycles, and show no evidence of discernible pumping-related trends due to the distance from large pumping centers. Similarly, the primary increase in groundwater pumping in the upper Klamath Basin has not occurred within Oregon spotted frog occupied sub-basins. The Service has little conclusive information at this time regarding groundwater pumping as a threat to Oregon spotted frogs.

(37) Comment: One commenter asserted that water management activities in the Glenwood Valley (the Middle Klickitat River sub-basin) may be artificially enhancing Oregon spotted frog habitat in that area because the landowners flood a significant portion of the valley to provide frost protection to the reed canarygrass they use for summer livestock forage and/or commercially produce. The commenter suggested that if water were allowed to runoff naturally, the area of available Oregon spotted frog habitat would be much smaller and would dry up sooner.

Our response: As explained in the Background and Summary of Factors Affecting the Species sections, water management in the Glenwood Valley is a complicated issue involving multiple landowners, including both public and private. Retention of water in locations that attract egg-laying behavior may create an "ecological trap" by trapping larvae and/or juvenile frogs if water is not retained until they are matured enough to move or if those locations are not hydrologically connected to permanent water via surface water along a gradual slope. These artificially flooded egg-laying areas may be creating population "sinks" and facilitating the decline of the population by diverting gravid females from higher quality, natural egg-laying locations. In addition, the current water management drains areas that in a natural setting might hold water throughout the year; whereas, currently, the surviving frogs are restricted to the ditch system, along with their predators, for a majority of the summer and winter. In the absence of additional compelling information, the Service continues to assert that water management is a threat to Oregon spotted frogs in the Middle Klickitat River sub-basin.

(38) Comment: One commenter asked that the Service clarify whether stormwater detention or retention facilities provide Oregon spotted frog habitat, including whether these facilities are beneficial or detrimental to the frog. (Oregon spotted frogs have been found within private storm drainage wetponds within Bend, Oregon.) The commenter further asked whether the State should continue to recommend that stormwater be directed away from frog habitat (as advised in Nordstrom and Miller 1997) if Oregon spotted frogs are shown to benefit from stormwater retention facilities.

Our response: The only known occurrence of Oregon spotted frogs using a stormwater retention pond occurs at the Old Mill within the City of Bend, Oregon. Year-round water is purposefully held within this particular pond because it serves as a "casting pond" for learning to fly fish. The Service does not have information to indicate that seasonally wet stormwater ponds are either a benefit or detriment to Oregon spotted frog populations that utilize the Deschutes River within the City of Bend.

In Washington State, Nordstrom and Milner (1997) remains the current accepted management practices guide. It clearly states, "stormwater runoff from urban developments should not be diverted into spotted frog habitats. Urban runoff often contains heavy metals and other pollutants that may affect frogs." Therefore, the information regarding controlling stormwater runoff away from frog habitat and the Washington Priority Habitat and Species Management Recommendations is accurate as presented.

Brand and Snodgrass (2010) concluded anthropogenic wetlands may be important to amphibian conservation in suburban and urban areas, but cautioned about the contaminants in the stormwater ponds. In addition, inferences from this study should be made very judiciously because the amphibian species studied were primarily terrestrial and only used the structures during the breeding season and their "natural" locations dried up before metamorphosis, so the structures were not providing for the essential needs of the associated amphibians and were essentially acting as a breeding sink.

The Service would not recommend that these types of facilities be constructed in or near Oregon spotted frog habitat because of the potential for creating ponds that do not remain wetted and could trap frogs or larvae, retain deeper water that attracts bullfrogs, or expose Oregon spotted frogs to contaminants.

(39) Comment: One commenter believed that the Service's discussion of development under Factor A was not well supported and argued that wetlands receive enough protections from Federal, State, and county regulations to be immune from the impacts of development.

Our response: The link between the frog's status and loss of wetlands is documented under both Factor A and Factor D. Ongoing loss of wetlands is predominantly attributable to development, including urban (housing and infrastructure) and agricultural. While some setbacks are required under existing regulations, not all "wetlands" are regulated in an equivalent manner, and not all counties or States have equivalent regulations. Additionally, not all Oregon spotted frog habitat is classified as "wetland" under county or State regulations, and thus the loss of these habitats are not accounted for under estimates of wetland loss. As discussed in our analysis under Factor D, we determined that the existing regulatory mechanisms are not sufficient to reduce or remove threats to Oregon spotted frog habitat, particularly habitat loss and degradation.

(40) Comment: One commenter believed the summary of the disease and predation section appeared to contradict the first paragraph of the section, pointing out that the first paragraph cites documentation that nonnative predaceous species are found in 20 of 24 sites while the summary states that at least one nonnative predaceous species occurs within each of the sub-basins currently occupied by Oregon spotted frogs.

Our response: These findings are discussed at different scales. Hayes et al. (1997, p. 5) documented at least one introduced predator in 20 of 24 individual sites surveyed from 1993-1997 in British Columbia, Washington, and Oregon. However, our summary is focused on the presence of nonnative predators at the sub-basin scale, not in individual sites; in other words, each occupied sub-basin has one or more sites with nonnative predators present. Further information on specific sites and sub-basins that are known to have predaceous nonnative species (made available within our Threats Synthesis Rangewide Analysis) is available online at both http://www.regulations.gov and the Washington Fish and Wildlife Service Office's Web site http://www.fws.gov/wafwo/osf.html.

(41) Comment: One commenter asserted that increases in the population of sandhill cranes in the Middle Klickitat River area and reports from local residents that indicate river otters have also moved back into the area may also be affecting the size of the Oregon spotted frog population.

Our response: We have no evidence to support or disprove that increasing populations of native species may negatively impact Oregon spotted frog populations in the Middle Klickitat River area. Cranes and otters may be playing a beneficial role for Oregon spotted frogs by preying on bullfrogs. We continue to recommend actions that address the impacts from introduced (nonnative) species, rather than native species.

(42) Comment: One commenter felt that the information provided under Factor C regarding Bd is inconsistent with Hayes et al. (2009), which posited that Bd was a contributor to the observed declines at Conboy Lake NWR and Trout Lake NAP. The commenter goes on to note that the referenced article also posited that the observed declines coupled with the unknown susceptibility of Oregon spotted frogs to Bd should be a cause for concern and then stated that this concern is heightened by the fact the Conboy Lake NWR is the only place where Oregon spotted frogs and American bullfrogs have successfully co-existed for over 60 years. The commenter's concern stems from data demonstrating that bullfrogs are known to carry Bd asymptomatically (citing Daszak et al. 2004; Garner et al. 2006); therefore the potential for Bd transmission within and among species at Conboy Lake NWR could be high.

Our response: We agree that Bd may be a cause for concern; however, there is no direct evidence that the declines in Conboy Lake area are attributable to Bd, and recent studies conducted by Padgett-Flohr and Hayes (2011) indicate that Oregon spotted frogs are less susceptible to Bd than many other frog species. The lack of co-occurrence with bullfrogs at Trout Lake NAP could potentially explain why that population is able to rebound, while Conboy Lake area does not, but it does not explain the increasing trend in the Sunriver population which has coexisted with bullfrogs for more than 40 years. There are a number of other contributing factors in the Trout Lake NAP that may explain the increasing population, such as significant improvement of the habitat conditions. Additional studies are necessary to determine whether Bd is a threat rangewide.

(43) Comment: One commenter requested clarification of which specific Urban Growth Area includes Fish Pond Creek because designation as an Urban Growth Area specifies the allowable permitted density of developments.

Our response: Fish Pond Creek is a tributary that flows directly into Black Lake from the east. The area where the frogs have been found breeding is within the Tumwater Urban Growth Area. Text has been added to the Factor D discussion in this rule to clarify this Urban Growth Area.

(44) Comment: Two commenters highlighted that shoreline, riparian, and wetland property owners throughout the PNW are regularly required through Federal, State, and local programs to improve fish habitat as mitigation for development and emphasized the involuntary nature of some of these mitigation programs. The commenters pointed out the apparent contradiction where the Service's proposed listing rule identifies such mitigation programs as having already contributed to the Oregon spotted frog's decline. The commenters stated his or her concern that a "dueling species" scenario between fish and frogs will not be resolved by listing the Oregon spotted frog as a threatened species, but will mean that property owners will face competing requirements stemming from the Act and other programs, and will be subject to potential liability on multiple fronts, either for refusing to engage in fish habitat mitigation (to avoid harming frogs), or for engaging in fish habitat mitigation activities that harm frogs. The commenters felt that a property owner's only alternative in such a situation may be to forgo using his or her property altogether and implied that the Service may be liable for a regulatory taking if property use restrictions resulting from enforcement of the Act deprive an owner of economic use.

Our response: We agree that habitat objectives for fish, and salmon species in particular, may in some cases contradict those for Oregon spotted frogs. In many cases, laws and regulations that pertain to retention and restoration of wetland and riverine areas are designed to be beneficial to fish species, resulting in the unintentional elimination or degradation of Oregon spotted frog habitat. In the "Summary of Existing Regulatory Mechanisms" under the Factor D discussion, we state that additional regulatory flexibility would be desirable for actively maintaining the areas essential for the conservation of the Oregon spotted frog. For example, grazing is an active management technique used to control invasive reed canarygrass, but CAOs in some Washington counties prohibit grazing within the riparian corridor. We also highlight the fact that the areas where these incompatibilities apply are limited in scope to four Oregon spotted frog-occupied sub-basins in Washington, a very small amount of area relative to the range of salmonids.

The Act does not allow the Service to refrain from listing a species in an instance such as this, where one species' habitat needs are different or incompatible with those of another listed species. In theory, two species that co-existed in the past should be able to co-exist in the present and future; however, due to human alteration of the naturally functioning ecosystem, human management of the ecosystem upon which these species depend now needs to accommodate the habitat needs of both species. As such, the incompatibilities and means to balance recovery objectives will be addressed in any future recovery plan for the Oregon spotted frog and are not relevant to a listing decision.

As for the commenters' assertion that limitations on the use of private property might effect a regulatory taking, the Act does not allow such considerations to influence a listing decision. In any event, the provisions of section 10 of the Act, allowing landowners to take listed species in accordance with an approved habitat conservation plan, are generally an effective means of resolving such issues without foreclosing all use of property.

(45) Comment: One commenter felt that our Factor D discussion places too much emphasis on the failures of existing regulatory mechanisms. The regulatory mechanisms are not as problematic as depicted in the text, and the whole section should be revised to better depict the protection provided by existing regulatory mechanisms.

Our response: As discussed in the introductory paragraph to the Factor D analysis, we examine whether the existing regulatory mechanisms are inadequate to address the threats to the species. We interpret this to include relevant laws, regulations, or mechanisms that may minimize any of the threats we described in the threat analyses under the other four factors, or otherwise enhance conservation of the species. This section only includes those laws, regulations, or mechanisms that we have found to be inadequate. It does not contain those laws, regulations, or mechanisms that we have found to be adequate or which do not address the specific threats to the species.

(46) Comment: One commenter stated that there is no evidence that water quality in the habitats occupied by Oregon spotted frogs is contaminated and asserts that because there is no evidence that water quality is affecting the populations in the Conboy Lake area or the Trout Lake NAP, the conclusion that water quality and contamination is a threat to the Oregon spotted frog across its range is not supported.

Our response: We have revised our conclusion about the extent of threats due to water quality. Reduced water quality is documented in a number of occupied sub-basins, and where this overlap occurs we consider poor water quality and contaminants to be threats to the Oregon spotted frog. Various parameters of water quality were identified as issues from British Columbia south to the Klamath Basin (see Factor E discussion). Specifically, the WDOE listed a Trout Lake Creek segment within known Oregon spotted frog areas as not meeting standards for fecal coliform, pH, dissolved oxygen, and temperature. We recognize that not all water quality parameters are equal and the standards set for fish may or may not be detrimental to Oregon spotted frogs. However, many of the parameters that we identified in association with water quality, such as pH and dissolved oxygen, are applicable, as is temperature when it is resulting in algal blooms and low oxygen levels (see discussion under the Life History section).

(47) Comment: One commenter felt that there was a conflict between the threat analysis conducted under Factor C and the cumulative threat analysis. The commenter requested clarification as to how the Service could cite Blaustein et al. (1999), which the commenter interpreted as concluding that Oregon spotted frogs were not affected by UV-B radiation exposure or contaminants, and then determine that UV-B radiation exposure and contaminants could negatively impact Oregon spotted frogs in the cumulative threats analysis.

Our response: Our threat analysis under Factor C did not say that Oregon spotted frogs are not affected by UV-B radiation, only that at present, the extent of population-level impacts from UV-B exposure is unknown. We highlight here that the Blaustein et al. 1999 study was conducted on eggs, but more recent work indicates that larvae (tadpoles) are more susceptible than embryos (Bancroft et al. 2008) and that UV-B radiation interacts synergistically with other environmental stressors. We also considered climate change as potentially playing a role in increased exposure to UV-B radiation if water depth at egg-laying and rearing locations is reduced. Our threat analysis also did not state that contaminants do not affect Oregon spotted frogs. Although we acknowledged that more ecotoxicology is warranted, the analyses provided a variety of impacts that contaminants can have on the species. Like UV-B radiation exposure, contaminants interact synergistically with other environmental stressors. Therefore, it is appropriate to include UV-B radiation exposure and contaminants in the cumulative effects analysis because of the complex interactions of stressors and the response Oregon spotted frogs may exhibit to varied combinations of these stressors.

(48) Comment: One commenter stated that the Service failed to sufficiently analyze whether the populations of Oregon spotted frogs constitute one or more distinct population segments (DPSs), particularly in the Upper Deschutes and Little Deschutes sub-basins. The commenter asserted that the Service would have a strong basis to find that these populations constitute one or more DPS given the sizable populations in these sub-basins, and, as such, it is premature to list these populations as threatened.

Our response: Congress has instructed the Secretary to exercise authority with regard to DPSs "* * * sparingly and only when the biological evidence indicates that such action is warranted" (Senate Report 151, 96th Congress, 1st Session). We evaluated whether any populations of the Oregon spotted frog constituted a DPS prior to our proposed listing rule; however, after conducting our threats analysis we concluded that the Oregon spotted frog is a threatened species across its range. Therefore, because we have determined that the Oregon spotted frog is threatened rangewide, there is no regulatory benefit in designating separate DPSs.

(49) Comment: One commenter noted that impacts from recreational access are not documented in the proposed listing until the section where the list of examples of activities conducted, regulated, or funded by Federal agencies is addressed. The commenter questioned whether or not recreational impacts constitute a real problem. The commenter further questioned whether or not river restoration should be included in this section, as Oregon spotted frogs are not a "riverine" species.

Our response: This list of examples of activities was provided to draw the Federal agency's attention to the types of activities that may require conference or consultation under section 7(a) of the Act; however, we are not aware that they are occurring or planned at this time. If they were to occur, recreation management actions, such as development of campgrounds or boat launches adjacent to or in Oregon spotted frog habitat, may result in impacts to the species or its habitat or both. Additionally, river restoration activities also may result in impacts to the species or its habitat or both because Oregon spotted frogs are closely tied to creeks and rivers, such as the Samish and Black Rivers in Washington and the Deschutes River in Oregon.

(50) Comment: The Deschutes Basin Board of Control (DBBC) requested a rule under section 4(d) of the Act that would not prohibit incidental take of Oregon spotted frogs during routine irrigation district activities, such as the storage, release, diversion, and return of water, if those activities are conducted in accordance with State law; and within ranges of storage, release, diversion, and return experienced since 1980, or within limits established in a HCP approved by the Service in accordance with section 10(a)(1)(B) of the Act. The DBBC also requested the 4(d) rule address the maintenance, operation, repair, or modification of existing district facilities if, among other requirements, these activities do not result in the direct physical modification of habitat occupied by the Oregon spotted frog or if these activities are addressed in an HCP. The DBBC requested that we provide another opportunity for public comment on our 4(d) rule determination before issuing a final rule.

Our response: We appreciate the DBBC's desire to consider conservation of Oregon spotted frogs in carrying out their ongoing activities. In our proposed listing rule, we indicated we are considering whether it is necessary and advisable to develop a 4(d) rule that would not prohibit take that is incidental to implementing a State comprehensive Oregon spotted frog conservation program, regional or local Oregon spotted frog conservation programs, and activities or efforts conducted by individual landowners that are outside of a more structured program but are still consistent with maintaining or advancing the conservation of Oregon spotted frog. Further, we indicated that we would consider specific information that would provide us a high level of certainty that a conservation program would lead to the long-term conservation of Oregon spotted frogs (see Consideration of a 4(d) Special Rule in the August 29, 2013, proposed listing rule).

Given the storage, release, and diversion of water in the Upper Deschutes River and the Little Deschutes River were identified in our proposed listing rule as sources of Oregon spotted frog habitat loss or modification, the information provided by DBBC did not provide the information we needed to evaluate the program's potential conservation benefits to the Oregon spotted frog. However, we have been working with the DBBC, and funding has been provided, to develop a HCP. If the HCP is finalized and permitted by the Service, it will likely authorize incidental take of Oregon spotted frog resulting from routine irrigation district activities, such as those described in their comment letter, while conserving the Oregon spotted frog consistent with the permitting requirements of section 10 of the Act. Such a permit would negate the need for coverage under a 4(d) rule. We encourage the DBBC to continue working with us to develop and finalize the HCP in order to authorize incidental take associated with these activities. Although we are not reopening a public comment period on the proposed listing, as requested by the DBBC, we may continue to consider developing a proposed 4(d) rule after this listing is finalized if we were to receive appropriate specific information that would provide us with a high level of certainty that such activities would lead to the long-term conservation of Oregon spotted frogs.

Summary of Changes From the Proposed Rule

We fully considered comments from the peer reviewers and from the public on the proposed rule to develop this final listing for Oregon spotted frog. This final rule incorporates changes to our proposed listing based on the comments that we received that are discussed above. We expanded our discussion of water quality to acknowledge maximum levels as being toxic to amphibians and provided maximum limits set by the EPA for human drinking water. We also expanded our water quality discussion to include information on the effects of low dissolved oxygen and revised our conclusion concerning the extent of threats due to water quality. We added text to the "Hydrological Changes" section in the Factor A discussion of this rule to reflect the potential of manmade barriers to hinder frog movement. We added language discussing the effects that soil compaction may have on water holding capacity and revised language in the Background and Summary of Factors Affecting the Species sections, where appropriate, to remove the term "early seral." We have updated the sub-basin information to include 2013 data where the new information expanded the distribution or significantly changed the minimum population estimate. Based on feedback from one of our peer reviewers, language regarding the number and distribution of the known Oregon spotted frogs in the Upper Deschutes River sub-basin has been revised. We have updated the Background section to include a short discussion of the indirect effects of Bti and methoprene on Oregon spotted frogs, and we added some text elsewhere to further explain our conclusion about parasite-induced malformations. We revised our discussion of reproduction to include additional uncertainty regarding the number of clutches of eggs a female may produce per year. We also added text to the Factor D discussion to clarify the boundaries of the Urban Growth Areas. In addition, we corrected several citations and made editorial corrections in response to comments.

Determination

Section 4 of the Act (16 U.S.C. 1533), and its implementing regulations at 50 CFR part 424, set forth the procedures for adding species to the Federal Lists of Endangered and Threatened Wildlife and Plants. Under section 4(a)(1) of the Act, we may list a species based on (A) The present or threatened destruction, modification, or curtailment of its habitat or range; (B) overutilization for commercial, recreational, scientific, or educational purposes; (C) disease or predation; (D) the inadequacy of existing regulatory mechanisms; or (E) other natural or manmade factors affecting its continued existence. Listing actions may be warranted based on any of the above threat factors, singly or in combination.

We have carefully assessed the best scientific and commercial information available regarding the past, present, and future threats to the Oregon spotted frog. Past human actions have destroyed, modified, and curtailed the range and habitat available for the Oregon spotted frog, which is now absent from 76 to 90 percent of its former range. The Oregon spotted frog populations within two of the sub-basins are declining, but the population trend in the other 13 sub-basins is undetermined. However, the Oregon spotted frog is extant in only 15 of 31 sub-basins where it historically occurred. In addition, the majority of remaining populations are isolated both between and within sub-basins, with minimal opportunity for natural recolonization. These isolated populations are, therefore, vulnerable to ongoing threats and extirpation, and threats are known to be ongoing or increasing across the range of the Oregon spotted frog, as summarized below.

Habitat necessary to support all life stages is continuing to be impacted and/or destroyed by human activities that result in the loss of wetlands to land conversions; hydrologic changes resulting from operation of existing water diversions/manipulation structures, new and existing residential and road developments, drought, and removal of beavers; changes in water temperature and vegetation structure resulting from reed canarygrass invasions, plant succession, and restoration plantings; and increased sedimentation, increased water temperatures, reduced water quality, and vegetation changes resulting from the timing, intensity, and location of livestock grazing. Oregon spotted frogs in all currently occupied sub-basins in British Columbia, Washington, and Oregon are subject to one or more of these threats to their habitat. Eleven of the 15 sub-basins are currently experiencing a high to very high level of habitat impacts, and these impacts are expected to continue into the foreseeable future.

Disease continues to be a concern, but our evaluation of the best scientific information available indicates that disease is not currently a threat to Oregon spotted frogs. At least one nonnative predaceous species occurs within each of the sub-basins currently occupied by Oregon spotted frogs. Introduced fish have been documented within each sub-basin; these introduced species prey on tadpoles, negatively affect overwintering habitat, and can significantly threaten Oregon spotted frog populations, especially during droughts. Bullfrogs (and likely green frogs) prey on juvenile and adult Oregon spotted frogs, and bullfrog tadpoles can outcompete or displace Oregon spotted frog tadpoles. In short, nonnative bullfrogs effectively reduce the abundance of all Oregon spotted frog life stages and pose an added threat to a species that has significant negative impacts rangewide from habitat degradation. Nine of the 15 occupied sub-basins are currently experiencing moderate to very high impacts due to predation by introduced species, and these impacts are expected to continue into the foreseeable future.

Lack of essential habitat protection under Federal, State, Provincial, and local laws leaves this species at continued risk of habitat loss and degradation in British Columbia, Washington, and Oregon. In many cases, laws and regulations that pertain to retention and restoration of wetland and riverine areas are a no-management (i.e., avoidance) approach, or are designed to be beneficial to fish species (principally salmonids), resulting in the elimination or degradation of Oregon spotted frog early-seral habitat. In other cases, no regulations address threats related to the draining or development of wetlands or hydrologic modifications, which can also eliminate or degrade Oregon spotted frog habitat. Therefore, degradation of habitat is ongoing despite regulatory mechanisms, and these mechanisms have been insufficient to significantly reduce or remove the threats to the Oregon spotted frog.

Many of the Oregon spotted frog breeding locations are small and isolated from other breeding locations. Due to their fidelity to breeding locations and vulnerability to fluctuating water levels, predation, and low overwinter survival, Oregon spotted frogs can experience rapid population turnovers that they may not be able to overcome. Low connectivity among occupied sub-basins and among breeding locations within a sub-basin, in addition to small population sizes, contributes to low genetic diversity within genetic groups and high genetic differentiation among genetic groups. Oregon spotted frogs in every occupied sub-basin are subject to more than one stressor, such as loss or reduced quality of habitat and predation. Therefore, the species may be more susceptible to the synergistic effects of combined threats, which may be exacerbated by climate change. The threat to Oregon spotted frogs from other natural or manmade factors is occurring throughout the entire range of the species, and the population-level impacts are expected to continue into the foreseeable future.

All of the known Oregon spotted frog occupied sub-basins are currently affected by one or more of these threats, which reduce the amount and quality of available breeding, summer, and overwintering habitat. While the risk to an individual site from each of these factors may vary, the cumulative risk of these threats to each site is high. This scenario is reflected in declining and/or small populations, which constitute the majority the Oregon spotted frog's remaining distribution. We find that Oregon spotted frogs are likely to become endangered throughout all or a significant portion of their range within the foreseeable future, based on the immediacy, severity, and scope of the threats described above. However, the best scientific and commercial information does not indicate at the present time that the existing threats are of such a great magnitude that Oregon spotted frogs are in immediate danger of extinction. Threats are not geographically concentrated in any portions of the species' range, and the species is extant and redundant at a number of localities within 13 of 15 sub-basins within British Columbia, Washington, and Oregon. One extant population remains in each of the Lower Deschutes River and Middle Fork Willamette sub-basins in Oregon. Egg mass surveys continue to document reproducing adults in most areas, although in at least two locations within the current range, Oregon spotted frogs may no longer be extant (i.e., the Maintenance Detachment Aldergrove site in British Columbia and the 110th Avenue site at Nisqually NWR in Washington).

The Act defines an endangered species as any species that is "in danger of extinction throughout all or a significant portion of its range" and a threatened species as any species "that is likely to become endangered throughout all or a significant portion of its range within the foreseeable future." We find that the Oregon spotted frog is likely to become endangered throughout all or a significant portion of its range within the foreseeable future, based on the immediacy, severity, and scope of the threats described above. The best scientific and commercial information does not indicate at the present time that the existing threats are of such a great magnitude that Oregon spotted frogs are in immediate danger of extinction, but we conclude that it is likely to become so in the foreseeable future. Therefore, on the basis of the best available scientific and commercial information, we determine that the Oregon spotted frog meets the definition of threatened in accordance with sections 3(20) and 4(a)(1) of the Act.

Significant Portion of the Range

The Act defines an endangered species as any species that is "in danger of extinction throughout all or a significant portion of its range" and a threatened species as any species "that is likely to become endangered throughout all or a significant portion of its range within the foreseeable future." A major part of the analysis of "significant portion of the range" requires considering whether the threats to the species are geographically concentrated in any way. If the threats are essentially uniform throughout the species' range, then no portion is likely to warrant further consideration.

The best available data suggest that, under current conditions, Oregon spotted frogs will likely continue to decline toward extinction. Having already determined that the Oregon spotted frog is a threatened species throughout its range, we considered whether threats may be so concentrated in some portion of its range that, if that portion were lost, the entire species would be in danger of extinction. We reviewed the entire supporting record for the status review of this species with respect to the geographic concentrations of threats, and the significance of portions of the range to the conservation of the species. Oregon spotted frogs currently occupy 15 sub-basins that are widely distributed, such that a catastrophic event in one or more of the sub-basins would not extirpate Oregon spotted frogs throughout their range. Based on our five-factor analysis of threats throughout the range of the Oregon spotted frog, we found that threats to the survival of the species occur throughout the species' range and are not significantly concentrated or substantially greater in any particular portion of their range. Therefore, we find that there is no significant portion of the Oregon spotted frog's range that may warrant a different status. Therefore, the species as a whole is not presently in danger of extinction, and does not meet the definition of an endangered species under the Act.

Available Conservation Measures

Conservation measures provided to species listed as endangered or threatened under the Act include recognition, recovery actions, requirements for Federal protection, and prohibitions against certain practices. Recognition through listing results in public awareness, and conservation by Federal, State, Tribal, and local agencies; private organizations; and individuals. The Act encourages cooperation with the States and requires that recovery actions be carried out for all listed species. The protection required by Federal agencies and the prohibitions against certain activities are discussed, in part, below.

The primary purpose of the Act is the conservation of endangered and threatened species and the ecosystems upon which they depend. The ultimate goal of such conservation efforts is the recovery of these listed species, so that they no longer need the protective measures of the Act. Subsection 4(f) of the Act requires the Service to develop and implement recovery plans for the conservation of endangered and threatened species. The recovery planning process involves the identification of actions that are necessary to halt or reverse the species' decline by addressing the threats to its survival and recovery. The goal of this process is to restore listed species to a point where they are secure, self-sustaining, and functioning components of their ecosystems.

Recovery planning includes the development of a recovery outline after a species is listed and preparation of a draft and final recovery plan. The recovery outline guides the immediate implementation of urgent recovery actions and describes the process to be used to develop a recovery plan. Revisions of the plan may be done to address continuing or new threats to the species, as new substantive information becomes available. The recovery plan identifies site-specific management actions that set a trigger for review of the five factors that control whether a species remains listed or may be delisted, and methods for monitoring recovery progress. Recovery plans also establish a framework for agencies to coordinate their recovery efforts and provide estimates of the cost of implementing recovery tasks. Recovery teams (composed of species experts, Federal and State agencies, nongovernmental organizations, and stakeholders) are often established to develop recovery plans. When completed, the recovery outline, draft recovery plan, and the final recovery plan will be available on our Web site (http://www.fws.gov/endangered), or from our Washington Fish and Wildlife Office (see FOR FURTHER INFORMATION CONTACT).

Implementation of recovery actions generally requires the participation of a broad range of partners, including other Federal agencies, States, Tribes, nongovernmental organizations, businesses, and private landowners. Examples of recovery actions include habitat restoration (e.g., restoration of native vegetation), research, captive propagation and reintroduction, and outreach and education. The recovery of many listed species cannot be accomplished solely on Federal lands because their range may occur primarily or solely on non-Federal lands. To achieve recovery of these species requires cooperative conservation efforts on private, State, and Tribal lands.

Following publication of this final listing rule, funding for recovery actions will be available from a variety of sources, including Federal budgets, State programs, and cost share grants for non-Federal landowners, the academic community, and nongovernmental organizations. In addition, pursuant to section 6 of the Act, the States of Washington, Oregon, and California will be eligible for Federal funds to implement management actions that promote the protection or recovery of the Oregon spotted frog. Information on our grant programs that are available to aid species recovery can be found at: http://www.fws.gov/grants.

Please let us know if you are interested in participating in recovery efforts for the Oregon spotted frog. Additionally, we invite you to submit any new information on this species whenever it becomes available and any information you may have for recovery planning purposes (see FOR FURTHER INFORMATION CONTACT).

Section 7(a) of the Act requires Federal agencies to evaluate their actions with respect to any species that is listed as an endangered or threatened species and with respect to its critical habitat, if any is designated. Regulations implementing this interagency cooperation provision of the Act are codified at 50 CFR part 402. If a species is listed subsequently, section 7(a)(2) of the Act requires Federal agencies to ensure that activities they authorize, fund, or carry out are not likely to jeopardize the continued existence of the species or destroy or adversely modify its critical habitat. If a Federal action may affect a listed species or its critical habitat, the responsible Federal agency must enter into consultation with the Service.

Federal agency actions within the species' habitat that may require conference or consultation or both as described in the preceding paragraph include, but are not limited to, management and any other landscape-altering activities on Federal lands administered by the U.S. Fish and Wildlife Service, USFS, BLM, and Joint Base Lewis McChord; actions funded or carried out by NRCS, USDA Rural Development, USDA Farm Service Agency, and USDA APHIS; issuance of section 404 Clean Water Act permits by the Corps; construction and maintenance of roads or highways by the Federal Highway Administration; construction and maintenance renewable and alternative energy projects and right-of-way corridors under U.S. Department of Energy and Bonneville Power Administration; and activities and infrastructure construction and maintenance associated with water storage and delivery under the purview of Bureau of Reclamation.

Examples of other activities conducted, regulated, or funded by Federal agencies that may affect listed species or their habitat include, but are not limited to:

(1) Vegetation management such as planting, grazing, burning, mechanical treatment, and/or application of pesticides adjacent to or in Oregon spotted frog habitat;

(2) Water manipulation, such as flow management, water diversions, or canal dredging or piping;

(3) Recreation management actions such as development of campgrounds or boat launches adjacent to or in Oregon spotted frog habitat;

(4) River restoration, including channel reconstruction, placement of large woody debris, vegetation planting, reconnecting riverine floodplain, or gravel placement adjacent to or in Oregon spotted frog habitat;

(5) Pond construction; and

(6) Import, export, or trade of the species.

Under section 4(d) of the Act, the Service has discretion to issue regulations that we find necessary and advisable to provide for the conservation of threatened species. The Act and its implementing regulations set forth a series of general prohibitions and exceptions that apply to threatened wildlife. The prohibitions of section 9(a)(1) of the Act, as applied to threatened wildlife and codified at 50 CFR 17.31, make it illegal for any person subject to the jurisdiction of the United States to take (which includes harass, harm, pursue, hunt, shoot, wound, kill, trap, capture, or collect; or to attempt any of these) threatened wildlife within the United States or on the high seas. In addition, it is unlawful to import; export; deliver, receive, carry, transport, or ship in interstate or foreign commerce in the course of commercial activity; or sell or offer for sale in interstate or foreign commerce any listed species. It is also illegal to possess, sell, deliver, carry, transport, or ship any such wildlife that has been taken illegally. Certain exceptions apply to employees of the Service, the National Marine Fisheries Service, other Federal land management agencies, and State conservation agencies.

We may issue permits to carry out otherwise prohibited activities involving threatened wildlife under certain circumstances. Regulations governing permits are codified at 50 CFR 17.32. With regard to threatened wildlife, a permit may be issued for the following purposes: For scientific purposes, to enhance the propagation or survival of the species, and for incidental take in connection with otherwise lawful activities. There are also certain statutory exemptions from the prohibitions, which are found in sections 9 and 10 of the Act.

It is our policy, as published in the Federal Register on July 1, 1994 (59 FR 34272), to identify to the maximum extent practicable at the time a species is listed, those activities that would or would not constitute a violation of section 9 of the Act. The intent of this policy is to increase public awareness of the effect of a listing on proposed and ongoing activities within the range of listed species. At this time, we are unable to identify specific activities that would not be considered to result in a violation of section 9 of the Act because the Oregon spotted frog occurs in a variety of habitat conditions across its range and it is likely that site specific conservation measures may be needed for activities that may directly or indirectly affect the species. The following activities could potentially result in a violation of section 9 of the Act; this list is not comprehensive:

(1) Introduction of nonnative species that compete with or prey upon the Oregon spotted frog, such as bullfrogs, green frogs, or warm or cold water fishes to the States of Washington, Oregon, or California;

(2) Modification of the wetted area or removal or destruction of emergent aquatic vegetation in any body of water in which the Oregon spotted frog is known to occur; and

(3) Discharge of chemicals into any waters in which the Oregon spotted frog is known to occur.

Questions regarding whether specific activities would constitute a violation of section 9 of the Act should be directed to the Washington Fish and Wildlife Office (see FOR FURTHER INFORMATION CONTACT).

Under section 4(d) of the Act, the Secretary has discretion to issue such regulations as he deems necessary and advisable to provide for the conservation of threatened species. Our implementing regulations (50 CFR 17.31) for threatened wildlife generally incorporate the prohibitions of section 9 of the Act for endangered wildlife, except when a rule promulgated pursuant to section 4(d) of the Act has been issued with respect to a particular threatened species. In such a case, the general prohibitions in 50 CFR 17.31 would not apply to that species, and instead, the 4(d) rule would define the specific take prohibitions and exceptions that would apply for that particular threatened species, which we consider necessary and advisable to conserve the species. The Secretary also has the discretion to prohibit by regulation with respect to a threatened species any act prohibited by section 9(a)(1) of the Act. Exercising this discretion, which has been delegated to the Service by the Secretary, the Service has developed general prohibitions that are appropriate for most threatened species in 50 CFR 17.31 and exceptions to those prohibitions in 50 CFR 17.32.

We have not proposed to promulgate a rule under section 4(d) of the Act for the Oregon spotted frog, and as a result, all of the section 9 prohibitions, including the "take" prohibitions, will apply to the Oregon spotted frog.

Required Determinations

National Environmental Policy Act (42 U.S.C. 4321 et seq.)

We have determined that environmental assessments and environmental impact statements, as defined under the authority of the National Environmental Policy Act (42 U.S.C. 4321 et seq.), need not be prepared in connection with listing a species as an endangered or threatened species under the Endangered Species Act. We published a notice outlining our reasons for this determination in the Federal Register on October 25, 1983 (48 FR 49244).

Government-to-Government Relationship With Tribes

In accordance with the President's memorandum of April 29, 1994 (Government-to-Government Relations With Native American Tribal Governments; 59 FR 22951), Executive Order 13175 (Consultation and Coordination With Indian Tribal Governments), and the Department of the Interior's manual at 512 DM 2, we readily acknowledge our responsibility to communicate meaningfully with recognized Federal Tribes on a government-to-government basis. In accordance with Secretarial Order 3206 of June 5, 1997 (American Indian Tribal Rights, Federal-Tribal Trust Responsibilities, and the Endangered Species Act), we readily acknowledge our responsibilities to work directly with tribes in developing programs for healthy ecosystems, to acknowledge that tribal lands are not subject to the same controls as Federal public lands, to remain sensitive to Indian culture, and to make information available to tribes. Oregon spotted frogs are not known to occur on Tribally owned lands. However, we provided information on our proposed and final listing rules to Tribal governments in Oregon and Washington where known Oregon spotted frog occurrences overlap with Tribal interests.

References Cited

A complete list of references cited in this rulemaking is available on the Internet at http://www.regulations.gov and upon request from the Washington Fish and Wildlife Office (see FOR FURTHER INFORMATION CONTACT).

Authors

The primary authors of this package are the staff members of the Washington Fish and Wildlife Office, Oregon Fish and Wildlife Office—Bend Field Office, and Klamath Falls Fish and Wildlife Office.

LIST OF SUBJECTS IN 50 CFR PART 17

Endangered and threatened species, Exports, Imports, Reporting and recordkeeping requirements, Transportation.

Regulation Promulgation

Accordingly, we amend part 17, subchapter B of chapter I, title 50 of the Code of Federal Regulations, as follows:

REGULATORY TEXT

PART 17 AMENDED

1. The authority citation for part 17 continues to read as follows:

Authority:

16 U.S.C. 1361-1407; 1531-1544; and 4201-4245, unless otherwise noted.

2. Amend § 17.11(h) by adding an entry for "Frog, Oregon spotted" to the List of Endangered and Threatened Wildlife in alphabetical order under AMPHIBIANS to read as set forth below:

§ 17.11 Endangered and threatened wildlife.

* * * * *

(h) * * *

| Species | Common name | Scientific name | Historic range | Vertebratepopulation whereendangered orthreatened | Status | When listed | Criticalhabitat | Special rules |

	*	*	*	*
*	*	*							
Amphibians							
	*	*	*	*
*	*	*							
Frog, Oregon spotted	Rana pretiosa	Canada (BC); U.S.A. (WA, OR, CA)	Entire	T	846	NA	NA
	*	*	*	*
*	*	*							

* * * * *

Dated: July 22, 2014.
Stephen Guertin,
Acting Director, U.S. Fish and Wildlife Service.
[FR Doc. 2014-20059 Filed 8-28-14; 8:45 am]
BILLING CODE 4310-55-P

Made in the USA
Coppell, TX
07 August 2022